Avalanche!

Evolution, God's Word, and The American Tragedy

Dr. Elliot Johnson

Avalanche!

Elliot Johnson

ISBN: 1-929478-55-0

Cross Training Publishing
317 West Second Street
Grand Island, NE 68801
(308) 384-5762

This book is manufactured in the United States of
America.

Published by Cross Training Publishing,
317 West Second Street

Grand Island, NE 68801

AVALANCHE!
Contents

ACKNOWLEDGMENTS • 5

FOREWORD • 7

INTRODUCTION • 9

SECTION I
AVALANCHE OF SIN AND JUDGMENT

Chapter One • 13
AN AVALANCHE OF SIN
Chapter Two • 18
AVALANCHE WARNING: THE LIE OF EVOLUTION
Chapter Three • 23
"FLAMING SNOWFLAKES"
Chapter Four • 28
THERE IS ALWAYS A REASON . . .
Chapter Five • 33
THE SNOW PILES UP
Chapter Six • 39
AFTERMATH OF AN AVALANCHE
Chapter Seven • 45
COLLAPSE OF AMERICAN CULTURE
Chapter Eight • 49
RELIGIOUS DEAD ENDS
Chapter Nine • 55
AMERICA: BEFORE AND AFTER JUDGMENT

SECTION II
LIGHT AND HOPE

Chapter Ten • 65
    LIGHT AT THE END OF THE TUNNEL
Chapter Eleven • 69
    THE CLEARLY MARKED TRAIL
Chapter Twelve • 75
    AVALANCHE AVOIDANCE
Chapter Thirteen • 80
    MONSTER SLIDES
Chapter Fourteen • 89
    OVERCOMING BLINDNESS
Chapter Fifteen • 93
    THE ONLY EYE WITNESS
Chapter Sixteen • 100
    Sovereignty of Our Creator
Chapter Seventeen • 103
    HOPE FOR SURVIVAL
Selected References • 109

Appendices:
    Appendix I - THE PROBLEM AND THE SOLUTION • 113
    Appendix II - GOD'S GREAT RESCUE • 117
    Appendix III - SPIRITUAL TEMPERATURE TEST • 121

Resources • 127
    ANSWERS IN GENESIS
    INSTITUTE FOR CREATION RESEARCH
    VISION FORUM MINISTRIES

Acknowledgments

None of us produces up to capacity without the help of others. This book was completed with the gracious assistance of many committed believers in Jesus Christ.

Special thanks is due to Heather Kinzinger, Carla Williams, and Kent Olney for their proofreading and encouragement; to John Weyant for his technical skills; to publisher Gordon Thiessen; and to my wife, Judy, for her patience and support.

Most of all, praise, honor, and glory are due to our Wonderful Lord Jesus, who spoke the world into existence and who reveals Himself to all who trust Him.

Elliot Johnson

AVALANCHE!

Evolution, God's Word, and the American Tragedy

Foreword

PERSONAL AND NATIONAL DISASTER is like a mountain avalanche. Though we think we can slide through life above temptation, sin is subtle and persistent. Once we yield to it, we become covered in a landslide of more and deeper sins. When enough people succumb, the moral structure of the nation collapses.

Many people believe America's moral decline began in the pulpits of her churches. The trumpet summoning Christians to battle for truth and righteousness gave an unclear call (I Corinthians 14:8). Misguided preachers began to doubt and then misinterpret the plain truth of God's Word. As a result, they "dressed the wounds of the people as though they were not serious" (Jeremiah 6:14). Needs stopped being met and people looked elsewhere for strength and counsel. Today, thousands regularly forsake churches for the golf course or the ski slopes on Sunday mornings. Many American churches are no longer taken seriously by most people. They are losing credibility by denying the historical accuracy of Genesis 1-11, which is the foundation of every major Biblical truth.

It has been said that God's Word will keep us from sin or sin will keep us from God's Word. This book is intended to help you to avoid personal disaster through the study and belief of Scripture. It is intended to identify the sin of unbelief and its consequences, affirm the Lord Jesus Christ as Creator and Sustainer, and bring renewed hope and motivation for living.

The only way to walk closely with Jesus Christ is to daily read, study, believe, and obey the Word of God. May God keep you from evil as you study His Word. And if you are already "buried alive" in purposelessness, may you rediscover purpose for living!

AVALANCHE!

Evolution, God's Word, and the American Tragedy

Introduction

MOUNTAIN AVALANCHES are caused by more than one factor. Seldom is one ingredient enough to cause a tragedy. Similarly, a variety of events have led to the publication of this book. America is in the midst of a war on terror. Authorities tell us conditions indicate further domestic attacks and there is widespread fear and turmoil. We have denied the traditional values that brought prosperity to previous generations. Many young people are lost in meaninglessness, having no purpose in life beyond immediate gratification. Drug use, teen sex, and suicide are epidemic in our culture. According to Dr. Norman Geisler, churches lose seventy-five percent of their youth groups after high school because they are not taught to defend the Christian faith. Recent (2002) surveys of American evangelical Christian youth conducted by Josh McDowell indicate that high percentages do not believe in absolute truth and other basics of the Christian faith. That same year, a George Barna poll confirmed that only thirty-two percent of American "Christians" and only nine percent of "Christian" teens believe morals are objective! This attitude is played out in our increasingly violent culture, as kids kill other kids in school. Many Christian leaders perceive the judgment of God upon America, with individual and national repentance our only hope.

As a college student, I majored in biology and later taught high school science. I was taught that man naturally evolved from "primordial soup" via apes over millions of years. But I had placed faith in the Bible and the Lord Jesus Christ, whom it reveals as Creator (John 1:1-3) in six days (Genesis 1). Was there any basis for faith in the God of Scripture at all? If the Bible was inaccurate about creation, there was no reason to believe it was accurate about anything! The Spirit of the Living God assured me His Word was true, but fellow students and teachers who had no faith in God were kept in darkness by Darwin's ideas. The God of the Bible was deprived of glory as Creator, besides being deemed irrelevant. If He did exist, who needed Him if all things occurred naturally by random chance? I began a thorough study of both science and Scripture. Not only did I have to know the truth, but Jude 3 told me to "contend for the faith once for all entrusted to the saints," and I Peter 3:15 said to "always be ready to give a reason" for my hope.

The Alaskan avalanche tragedy of Mike and Marty Phelps, former football players at Olivet Nazarene University, is a graphic illustration of the destruction in our nation. Though there are still many Bible-believing schools and churches where God's Word is taught and the Holy Spirit speaks, they are in the minority. These short chapters are intended to increase the comprehension of God's Word. The discussion questions at the end of each chapter are for families, small groups, and individuals to strengthen their faith and public witness. The "Temperature Test" in Appendix III will help measure spiritual knowledge and help identify where one stands in relation to God's Word. The God of the Scriptures is still active in America, no matter how hard His enemies work to remove every mention of Him. May He continue His work in and through you!

For His Glory,
Dr. Elliot Johnson

SECTION I

AVALANCHE
OF SIN AND JUDGMENT

Chapter 1
An Avalanche of Sin

MIKE AND MARTY PHELPS played football as hard as they worked in the woods. They hunted and fished together, played high school football in Pennsylvania, and then excelled at a small college in Illinois. On August 12, 1993, the twin brothers set out to hunt Dall sheep on Bernard Glacier in Alaska. Knowing that huge rams lived in the area, they had arranged to be picked up ten days later on a sand bar twenty miles down the glacier.

As Mike and Marty passed through the rugged surroundings of Wrangle St. Elias National Park, they were in awe of the surroundings. Feeling independent, self-reliant, and carefree, they hunted the drainage of the glacier, helping and encouraging each other as only twins can do.

On the fourth day of the hunt, they quietly climbed into a narrow, rugged valley. For three hours, they crept slowly from spot to spot, seeing several rams on the slopes. Jagged peaks reached to the solid blue sky above the steep canyon walls of ice and rock. They could see for miles. Then, suddenly, there was a small breaking sound. Before either could speak, rocks and ice blocks the size of cars rained down upon them. Mike was pounded flat, jammed into a small depression, but alive. Ten yards ahead of him, all was silent where he had last seen Marty.

Terror gripped Mike's heart as he called out to his twin brother through the dead, dark, frozen grave in which he found himself. Feeling as if he was trapped in a bad dream, Mike struggled furiously against the frigid mountain that had engulfed him. Everything was blurry and in slow motion. After clawing for about twenty feet, he saw a ray of light! Cold and wet, Mike slid toward the opening and out into brilliant sunlight — only to realize he was alone! His frantic calls for Marty were unanswered. Marty's body was never recovered.

Marty Phelps was entombed in a frigid Alaskan avalanche. His death was sudden and tragic. One moment Marty was full of energy and life, and the next moment he was gone. Mike Phelps moved toward the source of light and was saved from physical death.

Much like the avalanche that engulfed the Phelps twins, our country has been engulfed in an "avalanche" of unbelief. This avalanche is fatal for any person or nation who ignores God and fails to take His Word seriously. Many have slid down the slope of denying God's reality and revelation and worshipping self or science, the result of which is personal and national disaster.

Some people deny God's existence in an attempt to make themselves feel unaccountable. But logic tells us there is a God. We know God exists because of the law of cause and effect. Everything that exists didn't just happen. It was caused. A wristwatch cannot be made by putting the parts into a hat, shaking them up, and expecting them to assemble themselves! This universe is very complex. An intelligent Creator created and sustains it. Design implies a Designer!

We humans have the capacity to recognize moral right and wrong. Only God could put this conscience into us. We may not all agree on what is right and what is wrong, but all of us acknowledge there is such a distinction. Animals have no such awareness. One eats another and thinks nothing of it. But we know, instinctively, there is right and wrong because God has put such awareness into us. People of all times have had such convictions. Our moral consciousness is proof of God's existence.

The Light is Clearly Revealed

"The wrath of God is being revealed from heaven against all the godlessness and wickedness of men who suppress the truth by their wickedness, since what may be known about God is plain to them, because God has made it plain to them" (Romans 1:18-19).

God has clearly revealed Himself to even the most isolated, heathen person on the face of the earth. Psalm 19:1 says, "The heavens declare the glory of God; the skies proclaim the work of his hands." This proclamation goes on day after day in every language! Yet, most reject the knowledge of God and turn their backs upon the Almighty. They are without excuse. Therefore, God's wrath is revealed as He gives them over to the consequences of their sin. Occasionally, God supernaturally dispensed His judgment as He did with the worldwide flood (Genesis 7), with the raining of burning sulfur on Sodom and Gomorrah (Genesis 19), and with opening the earth up to swallow Korah's men (Numbers 16:32). Often, God allows sin to run its course and produce deadly disease and death (Romans 1:27). God *never* tolerates sin. He hates it!

People have no excuse for avoiding, ignoring, or denying God. No one who wants to know God and to enter His heaven will ever spend eternity in hell. The strongest, most persistent urge in people is not hunger or sex. It is to know God. But people suppress this urge, pushing it down like a basketball in a swimming pool. Humanity becomes ungrateful to God and worships created things. Their thinking becomes futile and foolish. The result is rationalism (evidenced by beliefs in evolution, atheism, and agnosticism) and idolatry (evidenced by materialistic selfishness). People have defied truth and dethroned God. They have believed Satan's lie ("You will be like God," Genesis 3:5). Paul says that to worship an idol, like a material thing, is to actually worship a demon (I Corinthians 10:20).

Eventually God lets people go their own way. What could be worse? Romans 1 describes the sequence. God "hands sinful man over" (vs. 24, 26, 28) in body, soul, and spirit to evil lifestyle "choices," and the sinner's behavior gets progressively worse. The opposite of evolution occurs: the sinner "devolves" into behavior lower than any animal. Animals don't kill for pleasure, but to eat. Animals do not have sex with those of the same sex, a sin that is the ultimate distortion of God's creative genius. It becomes impossible for such people to view anything as God intended. Their darkness runs very deep and they suffer in their own bodies the due penalty for their perversion (Romans 1:27).

God gives wicked men and women, who do not value the knowledge of Him, over to a depraved mind full of every kind of evil. They remain in slavery to their own lusts, and then seek poor substitutes (drug abuse, material things, prestige) to satisfy the urge for God. They become hard-hearted and past feeling (Ephesians 4:19).

Establishing an atmosphere of approval of such evil deeds is condemned by God (Romans 1:32). So is loving sin for sin's sake. Those who do such things *know* God is displeased and *know* they deserve death, however much they seek to rationalize or legalize their evil deeds.

Hope lies only in confessing and forsaking sin. Complete deliverance from this "avalanche of sin" is promised to all who believe God, move toward the light, and obey His Word!

RESCUE AND RECOVERY

THINKING IT THROUGH

How does worshiping self or science result in personal and national disaster?

How do you know there is a God?

What sins are Americans practicing and even promoting today?

LISTENING TO GOD

Romans 1:27

Ephesians 4:19

Romans 1:32

How does God's viewpoint change your thoughts and actions?

DIGGING OUT

Write out and pray the words of Psalm 51:1:

Chapter 2
Avalanche Warning:
The Lie of Evolution

WHEN AVALANCHE CONDITIONS appear predictable on a certain slope, officials may broadcast an avalanche warning. Such warnings are intended to keep skiers and hikers away from the area and to save their lives! Only a foolish adventurer would go into an area when a warning has been issued.

God has issued a severe warning to anyone who adds anything to or takes words away from His revelation (Revelation 22:18-19). When God's Word clearly tells us about His creative acts, we are in grave danger if we deny it.

A denial of God's Word results in denial of any absolute truth. When we deny God's absolute truths, we no longer have a basis for any moral code. People become their own gods in the religion of secular humanism. This is nothing more than self-worship. The idea of evolution is one of the foundational beliefs of self-worship. This "stronghold" is a way of thinking or acting that is contrary to God's will.

Ancient concepts of the universe varied greatly among ungodly cultures. The Egyptians imagined a bowl-shaped universe surrounded by mountains with Egypt in the center. To the Hindus, heaven was a pyramid standing on a curved earth, which rested upon elephants who stood upon a turtle which was supported by a serpent. Whew! The Persians said the universe was an island in an ocean filled with monsters. In medieval times, it was believed the universe was a star-studded dome above a flat earth. The most scientific belief is found in that ancient book, the Bible. Job 26:7 says the earth is suspended over nothing. When mankind rejects the Scripture and the supernatural power of God (Matthew 22:29), he descends into great darkness and will literally believe anything!

The Lie

II Thessalonians 2 describes the coming to earth of a powerful leader who represents himself as God and leads those who follow him to their destruction. Verse ten says they perish because they first "refused to love the truth." Therefore "God sends them a powerful delusion so that they believe the lie" concerning this Antichrist (vs. 11).

Belief in some form of evolution is as old as pagan religion. The modern lie that living beings evolved from "lower forms" of life was revived by an 18th-century rationalist named Erasmus, grandfather of Charles Darwin. Author Garrett Hardin writes that public opinion stood against Erasmus because of the evangelical movement led by John Wesley.[1] Rationalists believe in mankind's *rational* ability to determine truth, as opposed to mankind receiving truth as the supernatural *revelation* of God. The idea of evolution has enormous appeal to the natural man in his sinful state because he or she has a debased mind that *wants* to explain his or her origin outside of God. After all, if God created man, man is accountable to God! Natural man never arrives at truth apart from God's Spirit (I Corinthians 2:11-15). The truth is foolishness to the natural mind of man. He rejects the truth and embraces a lie about his origin and about God.

Early in the twentieth century, certain individuals educated in Europe and influenced by German rationalism began teaching in the seminaries of America. It did not take many such men working through the years to turn entire denominations of churches away from faith in God's Word. Today, evolution as a belief system has been established as a stronghold against the knowledge of God (II Corinthians 10:4-6). Though some intellectuals realize its utter implausibility, the stronghold can only be broken by faith in God and His Word.

One's belief concerning his or her origin will greatly determine his or her conduct. Therefore faith in a chance big bang, followed by millions of years of Godless evolution to form the universe and the complex human, plant, and animal life of today, has led to an avalanche of problems in every area of society. Belief in evolution lies at the foundation of the pagan religion called "secular humanism." Secular humanism is the belief that humanity is the highest authority. Essentially, it is the worship of humanity. Secular humanism glorifies nature with faith in natural selection to determine who and what lives and dies through "survival of the fittest." Evolution proclaims that humanity is getting better.

The Bible teaches that, since the fall of mankind, we are naturally dead in sins and the creation itself is dying (Romans 5:12, 8:20-21). As Dr. Jeremy Walter, head of the Engineering Analysis Design Department at Penn State University says, "In tenacious commitment to atheism, naturalistic evolution fashions the marriage of the false modern gods of Mother Earth and Father Time as an inferior substitute for the great and awesome Creator of the Scriptures."[2] The Bible says God created living things "according to their kind" (Genesis 1-2). Genetic *recombination* within kinds certainly has resulted in varieties (hybrids) of the dog "kind" or the cat "kind." But a dog remains a dog and never becomes a cat! The latent genes producing variety were present all the time. No natural law is known to give rise to new genetic information. God said His creation was very good. Mutations ("birth defects") are always for the worse. Never has one genetic mutation improved any living organism. Ardent evolutionists say well over ninety-nine percent of mutations are bad, instead of admitting one hundred percent are harmful and seeing their theory die! Evolution is a cruel, callous hoax that millions of years of death produce improved forms of life. The conflict occurs between naturalism and supernaturalism as the source of creation.

The lie of evolution is unscientific, for science by definition deals with what is observable and repeatable. Only God was there when He created everything there is! So, the issue becomes a matter of faith. Unbelieving scientists are willfully ignorant (II Peter 3:3-6). They see the evidence for creation by a Supernatural Creator, but refuse to acknowledge Him, replacing Him with belief in "millions of years" of genetic defects ("mutations") and chance ("randomness"). They place faith in random nothingness and worship at the altar of secular humanism. Others put faith in a sovereign, omnipotent God and worship Him. Whom do you worship?

RESCUE AND RECOVERY

THINKING IT OVER

What are the two belief systems about how truth is determined?

Define secular humanism. How do you experience it in school? On the job? Have you encountered it in church?

What evidence do you see that mankind is dead in sin? Are humans getting better by themselves?

LISTENING TO GOD

I Corinthians 2:11-15

Romans 5:12

II Corinthians 10:4-6

How does God's viewpoint change your thoughts and actions?

DIGGING OUT

Write out and pray the words of Psalm 19:1-4:

Chapter 3
"Flaming Snowflakes"

ONE OF THE SADDEST and most dangerous beliefs is that God originally created the universe, but allowed evolutionary processes to form life as we see it today. Labeled "theistic evolution," this is the most illogical position of all! A number of Christians believe in this attempt to reconcile what they think is science with Biblical teaching. They disbelieve their own Book, ignoring the truth that God's special creation is one of the main themes of Scripture. As Hank Hanegraaff says, "It is one thing to believe in evolution. It is quite another to blame God for it." He calls theistic evolution a contradiction in terms — like the phrase "flaming snowflakes." In his book *The Face*, Hanegraaff writes:

> An omnipotent, omniscient God does not have to painfully plod through millions of mistakes, misfits, and mutations in order to have fellowship with humans. Rather, He can create humans in a microsecond. If theistic evolution is true, Genesis is at best an allegory and at worst a farce. And if Genesis is an allegory or a farce, the rest of the Bible becomes irrelevant. If Adam did not eat the forbidden fruit and fall into a life of constant sin terminated by death, there is no need for redemption.[1]

In 1976, biologist Jacques Monod, an evolutionist who was given a Nobel Prize, said:

> [Natural] selection is the blindest, and most cruel way of evolving new species. . . . The struggle for life and elimination of the weakest is a horrible process, against which our whole modern ethic revolts. . . . I am surprised that a Christian would defend the idea that this is the process which God more or less set up in order to have evolution. [2]

Bible-believing Christians reject theistic evolution, for Hebrews 11:3 says, "By faith we understand that the universe was formed at God's command, so that what is seen was not made out of what was visible." God's creation was done "out of nothing" by the Lord Jesus Christ (John 1:1-3, 14; Colossians 1:16; Hebrews 1:2). Things did not evolve from preexisting material.

All the prominent founders as well as the leading proponents of evolution today scoff at theistic evolution. Leading evolutionist Sir Julian Huxley expressed the world's predominant viewpoint at the University of Chicago's Darwin Centennial Convocation in 1959 by saying, "In the evolutionary pattern of thought, there is no longer need or room for the supernatural. The earth was not created; it evolved. So did all the animals and plants that inhabit it, including our human selves, mind and soul, as well as brain and body. So did religion."[3] The two divergent belief systems are clear. Satan's strategy, as always, includes getting Christians to compromise the clear teaching of God's Word by promoting theistic evolution.

If theistic evolution is true, God's Word cannot be trusted, nor can Jesus. Jesus taught that creation of man and woman was at the beginning of creation and not four billion years later (Mark 10:6). He believed that God, not some natural process, created the world (Mark 13:19). If we cannot trust His Word in areas of biology, geology, and astronomy, how can we trust Him in matters of morality and salvation (John 3:12)? At stake is the credibility of Jesus Christ.

God is the God of order and grace. He is not wasteful or stupid. Evolution is a belief in wastefulness, purposelessness, extinctions, cruelty, and extermination of the weak. Mutations and death are a curse brought about because of sin, not God's means of creating. If millions of years of death and suffering before Adam's sin resulted in creation of new animals and humans, then God is responsible for death and suffering and men can justly blame Him when tragedy strikes. But God is not to blame for death and suffering. Sin caused death and suffering. The evolutionary model and the Biblical account totally contradict each other. One cannot believe both. Theistic evolution is contrary to God's nature and methods. All God does is perfect and complete. He does not experiment, create by trial and error, or fail the first time. The idea takes glory away from a supernatural God and gives it to imaginary natural processes. No rationalistic idea of humanity insults the creative genius of a sovereign, omnipotent Creator like the idea of theistic evolution. The phrase is as self-contradictory as the sentence "my brother is an only child," or "I can't speak a word in English (spoken in perfect English)"! It implies He is not powerful enough to create "out of nothing," nor wise enough to know what He wanted in the first place!

God has clearly told us how and why we came to be. The first person to question His Word was Satan. He began the confusion in Genesis 3:1, 4-5. "Did God say . . .?" Satan asked Eve. In other words, Satan was asking, "Did God really mean what He said? Maybe He had an alternative meaning. You have misinterpreted His teaching about the tree. You must have missed another possible, valid meaning!" WRONG! God's Word means exactly what it says and only what it says!

Compromise with false teaching never honors God. The fruit of compromising God's Word concerning origins becomes progressively worse. Unbelief in the literal Genesis account leads to theistic evolution, denial of Biblical inerrancy, liberalism, denial of the supernatural, and humanism.

Martin Luther (1483-1546) saw the danger of secular humanism in schools. In *America's God and Coun-*

try, William Federer quotes Luther as follows, "I am afraid that schools will prove to be great gates of Hell unless they diligently labor in explaining the Holy Scriptures, engraving them in the hearts of youth. I advise no one to place his child where the Scriptures do not reign paramount. Every institution in which men are not increasingly occupied with the Word of God must become corrupt.

Evolution contradicts the clear teaching of the Word of God. Could God have created using evolution? God can do anything consistent with His nature. Theistic evolution is false because it is contrary to God's nature. It is false because Genesis 1 tells us exactly how God created. Furthermore, the effects of evolutionary teaching upon society have always been harmful and degrading.

God said, "It is I who made the earth and created mankind upon it. My own hands stretched out the heavens; I marshaled their starry hosts" (Isaiah 45:12). Psalm 33:8-9 says He spoke the earth into existence. He pronounced all His creation "very good" after six days (Genesis 1:31). No sin had yet entered to defile it.

Nehemiah 9:6 adds, "'Blessed be your glorious name, and may it be exalted above all blessing and praise. You alone are the LORD. You made the heavens, even the highest heavens, and all their starry host, the earth and all that is on it, the seas and all that is in them. You give life to everything and the multitudes of heaven worship you. . . .'"

Jesus taught that the strong should *help* the weak. His teachings are the opposite of the "law of the jungle." Will you believe God's Word or will you be swallowed up under the avalanche of evolutionary deceit?

RESCUE AND RECOVERY

THINKING IT OVER

What is at stake for those who claim to believe in theistic evolution?

Who was the first one to question God and His Word?

What does the nature of the Living God tell you about creation?

LISTENING TO GOD

Mark 10:6

Genesis 3:1-5

Psalm 33:8-9

How does God's viewpoint change your thoughts and actions?

DIGGING OUT

Write out and pray the words of Psalm 40:16:

Chapter 4
There Is Always a Reason . . .

AVALANCHES ARE CAUSED. There are always several reasons why they occur. Among them are rapid changes in wind, temperature and snowfall, snow saturated with water, and loose underlying snow layers.

Why Some Trust Evolution

Just as there is always a reason for an avalanche, there is always a reason why some people trust evolution instead of Almighty God as their Creator. Sometimes there are multiple reasons.

First, they have been told it is factual and they have never studied the evidence for themselves. The intense evolutionary propaganda of the last seventy years has worked. Like Hitler said, "If you tell a lie long enough and loud enough and often enough, the people will believe it." He considered evolution a key to his master race theory. Marx, Stalin, and Hitler knew this ideology justified their extermination of the "unfit" in their desire to enslave the masses and form a new world order.

Second, some people give assent to evolution for prestige or for financial reasons. It is extremely difficult to obtain or retain a teaching position in a state university if one opposes this sacred cow. Peer pressure and desire for acceptance by the world is enormous. Even many Christian universities now give more respect to the vain ideas of educated men who are far from God than they give to God's own Word! To be accredited by the world is highly valued by many. Some are sincerely convinced that the Genesis account is allegory, myth, legend, or hyperbole and that secular science is authoritative. When they perceive a conflict, they put faith in this false science and reject the Word of God. This deception is subtle. How dare we discount God's Word! Isaiah 2:22 puts man and his ideas in perspective when compared to God's Word: "Stop trusting in man, who has but a breath in his nostrils. Of what account is he?"

Third, many people have spiritual reasons for accepting evolution. If there is no God who designed and sustains everything, they do not have to give an account to God when they die. People get very uncomfortable when they think of answering to such a powerful Creator upon their death. If evolution is true, we can live like animals and not pay the eternal consequences. We can justify any behavior if it is to survive or improve our own lives (abortion, euthanasia, extermination of "undesirables"). The law of the jungle becomes the law of the streets and schools when evolution is applied to society.

Faith in evolution to explain origins is a disaster. Tenets of this "religion" have been disproved over and over. New species do not develop. Some species go extinct. There are no definitive intermediate forms of life leading from one species to another. Outright deception, such as the 1999 hoax reported by a national magazine of a missing link (a "feathered dinosaur"), has often been used by evolutionists. "Nebraska Man," used as proof of evolution in the 1925 Scopes Trial, was later discovered to be constructed from the tooth of an extinct pig. "Piltdown Man" was an ape's jaw filed down to fit a human skull — a deliberate fraud. "Neanderthal Man" is simply an old man with arthritis. "Cro-Magnon" is 100 percent human. The "geologic column," invented in the early 1800s, is fictitious as presented in many school textbooks. The worldwide flood and earthquakes in Noah's time, with subsequent erosion, sedimentation and contortion of earth's crust much better explain the layers of the Grand Canyon. The rapid burial of plants and animals in the flood (not their decay) caused fossils to be preserved and coal to be formed under the enormous water pressure. The worldwide flood is mentioned in literature of various peoples of the ancient world, and in Genesis 6-8. It completely destroys the belief in uniformitarianism, the idea that natural processes have proceeded at the same rate over millions of years (II Peter 3:3-7).

Evolutionary belief is opposed to the second law of thermodynamics, which states that every system left to itself becomes more disordered. Things actually "devolve" from complex to simple. The universe is winding down, not gaining energy. It is wearing out (Isaiah 51:6; Psalm 102:25-26) and decaying (Romans 8:21). Evolutionary belief must be accepted by faith, and as such is a false "religion." The law of this religion is not science based upon fact.

Charles Darwin had no college degree in science. His degree was in theology, but he was an apostate (fallen away) who, according to biographer James Moore, was consumed with bitterness toward God because of the death of his daughter Annie. In 1859, he publicized the ideas of evolutionists before him, merely dressing ancient paganism in modern clothing. Evolution is merely worship of natural forces in place of the Creator, as described in Romans 1:21-25. The Scopes Trial in the 1920s focused much public attention upon evolutionary belief. Adolf Hitler adopted and promoted its precepts in the 1930s, for they fit his political philosophy perfectly. When communists engulfed much of the world, as they took over nations they immediately taught evolution to destroy moral authority and replace it with the authority of the state. America's religious leaders rejected

Scripture in deference to evolution's popularity among scientists, and when Russia launched a satellite named Sputnik in the late 1950s, we became alarmed. Science began to be greatly emphasized in schools. Educators smuggled evolution into every area of science. The project was called the "Biological Sciences Curriculum Study." Today, public school policy is still dominated by Darwinian evolution.

Interestingly, as the effects of evolutionary teaching achieve their greatest influence, the theory is losing credibility among some leading scientists. As quoted in *Advocate* (1984), one leading French scientist, Dr. Louis Bounoure, calls it a "fairy tale for grown ups." According to Dr. Colin Patterson, senior paleontologist for the British Royal Museum:

> For over twenty years I thought I was working on evolution. . . . [But] there was not one thing I knew about it. . . . So for the last few weeks I've tried putting a simple question to various people and groups of people. Question is: "Can you tell me anything you know about evolution? Any one thing? Any one thing that is true?"
>
> I tried that question on the geology staff at the Field Museum of Natural History and the only answer I got was silence. I tried it on the members of the Evolutionary Morphology Seminar at the University of Chicago, a very prestigious body of evolutionists, and all I got there was silence for a long time. And eventually one person said, "Yes, I do know one thing — it ought not to be taught in high school."[1]

Christians need not fear an objective study of evolution. The more facts we learn, the more preposterous evolution sounds! The tragedy is that while some atheistic scientists are aware of evolution's illogical and desperate condition, the public is still pounded with the idea in schools and museums that humanity evolved from a big bang or primordial soup over millions of years!

RESCUE AND RECOVERY

THINKING IT THROUGH

What does the outright deception of past evolutionary proponents say about their theory?

Why do so many people say they believe in evolution? What do you believe? What do your friends believe?

If so many scientists are becoming skeptical of evolutionary theory, why do you think it is still taught as fact in schools?

LISTENING TO GOD

II Peter 3:3-7

Romans 8:20-21

Isaiah 2:22

How does God's viewpoint change your thoughts and actions?

DIGGING OUT

Write out and pray the words of Psalm 12:1-2:

Chapter 5
Glacier Building and Collapse

MT. HUASCARAN RISES 6,700 meters high and is situated near the north end of the Andes in Peru. On January 10, 1962, an estimated three million cubic meters of snow and ice fell vertically from the glacier at the summit, for almost one kilometer! The impact formed a dense cloud of particles which sped down a valley with enormous speed and energy. Boulders, debris, and mud enlarged the mass to thirteen million cubic meters as it bore down on the small town of Ranrahirca and six other villages. All were destroyed and a river was dammed when the avalanche came to rest. But one thing led to another, for the debris dam was broken by the rising river, causing a disastrous flood which wrecked all the bridges downstream. Four thousand people were killed over a distance of 20 kilometers in only seven minutes, making the average velocity of the avalanche 170 kilometers per hour.

Like the build-up of snow on a glacier, the effects of unbelief are cumulative until the inevitable collapse of society. But before we discuss the consequences of our sin, we need to take a quick trip through history.

Before the Snowfall

Adam and Eve were created fully mature and very intelligent. They were creationists! They knew God, but disobeyed anyway! The "snowfall" of sin in humanity began with them. Almighty God was not taken by surprise. He had a plan of redemption in place and He began to reveal it immediately (Genesis 3:15).

Man's thoughts and intents soon became so evil, God had to destroy every living thing in a worldwide flood. Otherwise, His plan would have been thwarted. Only eight people, the animals on the ark, and the animals that live in the sea survived to reproduce His creation. The Great Flood, with accompanying earthquakes, explains much observable phenomena today, including the Grand Canyon, various layers of sediment which have hardened, and many fossils. After the flood, man refused to disperse, so God supernaturally divided mankind by language at the Tower of Babel. The isolated gene pools led to physical differences among people groups. Genetic information was *lost* to some groups, but never *gained*. (*Loss* of genetic information could also account for the virulence of some bacteria and viruses *after* the fall of man.)

Next, God selected a man, Abraham, through which to bless the world with the Savior, Jesus Christ. God gave us His Son, the living Word, and the supernaturally inspired written Word to save all who trust Him.

But Satan was not finished in his efforts to dethrone God. Satan causes God pain by attacking God's beloved human race. When he cannot *beat* them, he tries to *join* them! In 320 A.D., the Roman emperor Constantine made Christianity the state religion. Temples, idols, and shrines to almost every god in the pantheon of religion filled the streets of Rome. Instead of destroying these centers of idol worship, the Church rededicated them to Christianity, chiseled the names of pagan deities off statues, and replaced them with the names of the apostles, Jesus, and Mary! One hundred years later, a man named Augustine introduced man's wisdom along with God's wisdom as a way of discovering truth. In the book, *Are We Living in the End Times?*, Tim LaHaye and Jerry Jenkins write, "although he did not intend it, his spiritualizing of Scripture eventually removed the Bible as the sole source of authority for correct doctrine. At the same time, the Scriptures were kept locked up in monasteries and museums, leaving Christians defenseless against the invasion of pagan and humanistic thought and practice."[1]

Toleration of heresy resulted in dominance of heresy, and the torture and murder of Bible-believing Christians followed in the Dark Ages. LaHaye continues, "Their destruction so angered skeptics like Voltaire and Rousseau that they became anti-Christian thinkers and began to propagate an atheistic socialism born out of French skepticism, which ultimately merged with German rationalism. Today, their intellectual descendants champion a philosophy called 'secular humanism.'" In many mainline churches, the gospel is the "social gospel," characterized by the denial of Christ's virgin birth, His sinlessness, His deity, and His bodily resurrection. These false teachers also deny the depravity of man and the inerrancy of Scripture.

True science never contradicts Scripture. Many of the founders of modern science were Bible-believing Christians who believed that the universe, life, and humanity were created directly and specially by Almighty God. The scientific revolution received a huge boost from the Protestant Reformation. Leonardo daVinci (1452-1519) is more widely known as a great painter, but many consider him to be the founder of modern science. He was a serious believer in Christ and the Scriptures, as were Johann Kepler, Francis Bacon, Blaise Pascal, and Robert Boyle. Others who believed the Bible when it says God created life were Galileo, Robert Hooke, William Harvey, and Nicholas Copernicus.[2,3] Sir Isaac Newton, judged by many to be the greatest scientist who ever lived, wrote strong papers defending the six-day creation, the worldwide flood, and the Bible. Carolus Linnaeus, father of taxonomy, had great respect for the Scriptures and attempted to equate his "species" category with the "kinds" of the Bible. Therefore, he believed in the fixity of species." Though there were many other notable scientific Christians, the tide of unbelief rose. Evolutionary ideas and skepticism of the supernatural were around since antiquity, but men like Benedict Spinoza, Emmanuel Kant, Rene Descartes, and LaPlace turned many to pantheism, deism, and atheism. Evolutionists began to gain a hearing through Jean Baptiste Lamarck (1744-1829) in the early 1800s. People were becoming skeptical of Scriptural authority. It was starting to snow.

The Blizzard

Ironically, it was Bacon (1561-1626) who claimed it was possible to believe God and Scripture in matters of soul and spirit and in "science" for matters of the physical world. Once this view gained acceptance, Christianity was reduced to a "pie-in-the-sky" religion and credibility was lost.

When Darwin (who had no degree in science) published his theory of natural selection, it was like a dam breaking. It was only a few short years before much of the scientific world capitulated to unbelief. Even most churches jumped on the evolutionary bandwagon, compromising their beliefs. A tidal wave of humanism, socialism and communism followed — all based upon evolution. Creationists like Baron Kelvin, Louis Pasteur and Louis Agassiz opposed the movement, but most universities and even a number of seminaries abandoned Biblical Christianity. The blizzard was in full force.

In his book *The Face*, Hank Hanegraaff says that "more consequences for society hinge on the issue of human origins than any other issue."[4] You see, Darwin's views undermined the foundation of Christianity. Blind, random chance replaced God's purposeful, intelligent design for all living things. Without Adam and Eve and the fall into sin, who needs the redemption provided by the cross of Christ? Fredrick Nietzsche, who provided the philosophical framework for Hitler's Germany, predicted that the death of God in the nineteenth century would ensure the bloodiest century in human history in the twentieth century. His philosophy was evil, but his prediction proved accurate.

RESCUE AND RECOVERY

How does Satan attempt to "join" you when he cannot seem to "beat" you?

What are the results in your life of tolerating false teaching? How can you be firm but gentle when confronted with untruth?

How was the twentieth century the bloodiest in history? What do you think is ahead in the twenty-first century?

LISTENING TO GOD
I Timothy 4:1

Galatians 1:6-9

II Thessalonians 2:15

How does God's viewpoint change your thoughts and actions?

DIGGING OUT
Write out and pray the words of Psalm 25:4-5:

Chapter 6
Aftermath of an Avalanche

THE AFTERMATH OF AN AVALANCHE is devastating. Entire villages have been buried. Thousands of people have been swallowed up in monstrous floods of snow.

The aftermath of man's denial of God and His Word to embrace the religion of secular humanism is even more devastating. Evolutionary teaching concerning humanity's origins is an important part of the religion of secular humanism.

Racism

Secular humanism and evolutionary theory have been used to justify racism. Darwin called Caucasians the "higher civilized races." The subtitle of his book *Origin of Species* was "The Preservation of Favored Races in the Struggle for Life." He gave respectability to racism. Aldus Huxley had equally racist views against black people. Adolf Hitler and Karl Marx carried their evolutionist views to a logical conclusion: Natural selection dictated that only the fittest survived. They claimed superiority, and they sought to eliminate the unfit. As atheist Sir Arthur Keith wrote in *Evolution and Ethics* (1947), "The German Führer . . . is an evolutionist; he has consciously sought to make the practice of Germany conform to the theory of evolution."[1]

The truth is, we all came from Adam and Eve, who were created by God and placed in the Garden of Eden. All of us are related! Physically, there is only *one* race: the human race! We are all "one blood." The amount of melanin in one's skin is no more significant than his or her place of birth. We are of equal value before God. Christian leaders could greatly reduce racism if they would teach that all of us came from Adam and Eve and we are valued equally by God.

The conflict between people because of differences in skin color is a *sin* problem, not a *skin* problem. Our sinful nature causes us to look down upon those who are different from us. This is true of both white sinners and black sinners. It is also true of Hispanic, Semitic, and Oriental sinners. The Bible teaches that the root problem of all mankind is sin.

The genetic code for all mankind came from Adam and Eve and was passed on through the eight survivors on Noah's ark. More than one gene determines skin color through pigments produced. Melanin is the major pigment. The presence of more melanin produces darker skin, which protects us from ultraviolet rays and skin cancer. The absence of melanin means light skin, which allows sun to penetrate, producing Vitamin D. Differences in people result from a recombination of genes already present in Adam and Eve. "Mid-brown" parents can produce the entire range of colors in one generation! Most people in the world are "mid-brown."

Skin color is not the most significant divider of people. Language is. God instantly separated people by *language* at Babel (Genesis 11). He wanted them to spread over the earth. If the very black people who carried no genes for "lightness" married one another and migrated to an area where their children could not marry people of lighter color, a pure black line would exist until recombined with the very light-skinned people. It would be likewise if the illustration were reversed. There has been so much remixing of people groups over the years that it is difficult to know from which of Noah's sons (Shem, Ham, or Japheth) many individuals have descended!

In Case You Didn't Know

Presently, white-skinned people dominate developed nations, but in the past, it may have been the opposite. African nations like Egypt were very advanced in the past, while Europeans lived in caves and forests! Years ago, God flooded the earth, destroying every human being except the eight people in Noah's ark. We have all descended from Noah's sons. The family line of Shem became the Semites (Jews and Arabs). From the family line of Ham — presumed black-skinned — came Cush, followed by Nimrod and Mizraim, followed by the Egyptians, followed by the Libyans and Canaanites, of whom was Rahab. The family line of Japheth moved mostly north and gradually became more light-skinned. Today, all three lines have mixed, so we have every shade of skin genetically possible. The Bible classifies people on the important issue: Whether or not they love and serve God! It rarely mentions skin color, a relatively insignificant matter in God's eyes.

In America's white-dominant culture, it is interesting to rediscover long-ignored facts about black people in Scripture. Genesis 41 tells us that Joseph married an Ethiopian woman who bore Ephraim and Manasseh. These fathers of two tribes of Israel were part black! Numbers 12 says Moses married Zipporah, a Cushite whose father, Jethro, was a convert to Judaism. When Moses' sister Miriam grumbled about this interracial marriage, God disciplined her with leprosy!

King David's great-grandmother was Rahab, a Canaanite from the line of Ham (father of black descendants). His grandmother was Ruth, a Moabite (another Canaanite tribe). We do not know his features or shade of skin, but David had enough black ancestry to be called "black" if he lived in America today!

Romans 1:3 reminds us that Jesus Christ "as to His human nature" was a descendent of David. This had to happen through Mary. Joseph became Mary's husband, though he was not the father of Jesus. But Mary was Jesus' mother, and she was *also* of the ancestry of David! Jesus' genealogy is given in Matthew 1 and Luke 3 which, incidentally, traces a line of people all the way back to Adam, a real person and not a myth, legend, or allegory. Included in his family tree are Rahab, Bathsheba (daughter of Sheba), and Ruth. Clearly, Jesus had some black ancestry.

We know that the Ethiopians are dark-skinned. The Shulamite woman in the Song of Solomon was black and beautiful. Phinehas means "the Negro" and Kedar means "very black." The prophet Zephaniah descended from Cush (black). Evidently, many Jewish people are descendants of Cush (Zephaniah 3:10). At least the historians Josephus, Plutarch, and Tacitus thought many Jewish people were black. Egypt is called the "land of Ham" (Psalm 78:51), and evidently it has a rich black history. Both Augustine and Tertullian, early Christian leaders, were evidently black.

If we have black or brown skin, we are blessed by a great heritage. We must be thankful to a wonderful God for His wisdom in giving us color! Americans with white skin have been placed in a dominant culture and must never look down upon anyone who has less advantage today. Jesus would have us elevate the oppressed. Pictures illustrating Bible stories with white photos make it easier for whites to identify with the characters. Sometimes we incorrectly equate white with "right or "good" and black with "wrong" or "bad." Some of us need an attitude adjustment! Black people can read whites like a book. They know whether or not white people see them as people and love them. Likewise, white people read whether a black person sees them as people. No wonder the Black Muslims incorrectly get away with telling converts that Christianity is for whites only. We need to understand and appreciate the dignity and personhood of every man, woman, and child. It has been said that every black person in America remembers the day when he or she realized there was a different set of rules for black people. May this double standard stop now! We can stop it with an attitude of love.

Christianity is for all people. Jesus Christ, the Creator, died and arose for everyone. Character counts. Skin color is highly variable. God loves variety and He loves all equally.

RESCUE AND RECOVERY

THINKING IT THROUGH
How and why were people originally separated by God?

What is your feeling toward people with a different skin color than yours? How does your attitude need adjustment?

For whom did Jesus die? Whites? Blacks? Browns? Reds? Yellow-skinned people?

LISTENING TO GOD
Colossians 3:11-14

James 2:1-9

I Timothy 5:21

How does God's viewpoint change your thoughts and actions?

DIGGING OUT
Write out and pray the words of Psalm 41:1:

Chapter 7
Collapse of American Culture

ON FEBRUARY 7, 2002, rescue workers labored in bitter cold and fierce winds to free nearly 500 people trapped by an avalanche in the Salang Tunnel, the world's highest at 11,034 feet. The tunnel is located in the Hindu Kush Mountains north of Kabul, Afghanistan. Temperatures plunged to minus forty degrees and winds reached fifty-five miles per hour. People were buried in cars and trapped inside the tunnel. Most of the avalanche protection structures hanging over the road had been collapsed by years of war. Four people died in the disaster.

It is not the Scriptures, but years of evolutionary dogma that is the basis for the degradation of women, rejection of morality, and devaluation of human life in American society. Such teaching has collapsed America's "culture protection" structures and attempted to justify sin.

Degradation of Women

Darwin wrote:

> [Man] attains a higher eminence, in whatever he takes up, than can women — whether requiring deep thought, reason, or imagination, or merely the use of the senses and hands. If two lists were made of the most eminent men and women in poetry, history, painting, sculpture, music (inclusive of both composition and performance), history, science, and philosophy, the two lists would not bear comparison. We may also infer, from the law of the deviation from averages . . . [that] the average mental power in man must be above that of women. [1]

The father of social psychology, Gustave Le Bon, was Darwin's disciple. He wrote:

> [Even in] the most intelligent races [there] are large numbers of women whose brains are closer in size to those of gorillas than to the most developed male brains. This inferiority is so obvious that no one can contest it for a moment; only its degree is worth discussion . . . . Women represent the most inferior forms of human evolution and . . . are closer to children and savages than to an adult, civilized man. They excel in fickleness, inconstancy, absence of thought and logic, and incapacity to reason. Without a doubt, there exists some distinguished women, very superior to the average man, but they are as exceptional as the birth of any monstrosity, as for example, of a gorilla with two heads. Consequently, we may neglect them entirely. [2]

Rejection of Morality

A few years ago, an American president engaged in gross sexual acts with a White House intern — and lied about it! Some Darwinian biologists applied their evolutionary dogma to explain his immoral behavior. Larry Witham reported that the genetic program handed down by human evolution was "to have as much sex with as many females as possible in the Darwinian quest for heredity survival." Biological historian Michael Ruse said, "What Darwin says is that the most dominant male gets the first crack at the women. In that sense, I find Mr. Clinton's behavior absolutely normal, not normal in the sense that I approve of it, though." [3]

Human Life Devalued

A culture that fails to value human life is doomed. Belief in the killing of unborn babies and of older folks "past their usefulness" follows the evolutionary mindset. If an unborn baby is just a developing blob of tissue, he or she can be destroyed anytime before birth without conscience. If a human embryo is not a person, but a lower life form, it can be destroyed for its stem cells. If an adult is no longer "fit," why let him or her live? But if the unborn baby is known by God (Psalm 139:13-16) and his or her days are planned by God, those who murder that baby must deal with Almighty God! If an adult is God's creation, he or she is valuable and God has appointed a time for him or her to die (Hebrews 9:27). It is now legal in America to kill an unborn baby, carve up the body, and use the tissue for research. We conduct a brisk business in body parts of babies, and we are debating euthanasia, the "mercy killing" of older adults. If evolution is true, we should not be alarmed. But if God is Creator, we should be deathly afraid of an avalanche of God's judgment!

Abortion is the ultimate child abuse, but kids outside the womb face hazards, too. Too many Americans do not have time for children anymore. They are unwilling to sacrifice pleasure for their kids' sake. Abuse of living children is rampant.

The devaluation of human life is being lived out on American streets every day. Our children play video games where the winner racks up points by killing. They watch murder glorified in movies, further desensitizing them to an expanding culture of death. Drive-by shooters and calculating snipers terrorize us and we wonder what causes them to kill with impunity in real life. How can we be so dull of understanding? We have turned away from God and the value He places on human life. What will it take to cause us to turn back? What must Jesus, who loved children, think of our society of death? He must judge us!

RESCUE AND RECOVERY

THINKING IT THROUGH

What would you say to a friend who was considering an abortion?

Have you known anyone who had an abortion? How did killing her unborn baby affect her? What hope does the Bible hold out to her in I John 1:9?

What do you think about the killing of older people (euthanasia) who have "outlived their usefulness"?

LISTENING TO GOD

Psalm 139:13-16

Exodus 20:13

James 2:11

How does God's viewpoint change your thoughts and actions?

DIGGING OUT

Write out and pray the words of Psalm 80:3:

Chapter 8
Religious Dead Ends

CLIMBERS SCALE MT. EVEREST in many ways. But there is only one way to know the true and living God. That way is through the Lord Jesus Christ. All human religions are false and lead to dead ends and death. We will now examine the world's major dead ends.

Islam is the world's fastest-growing religion. Founded by Mohammed around 610 A.D. in Mecca, Saudi Arabia, Islam promotes a god called "Allah." He is depicted as an unloving and severe judge. Muslims deny the crucifixion of Jesus Christ. They believe humans are basically good but need guidance. They teach that good deeds must outweigh bad deeds to reach heaven and avoid hell. God's mercy may help, but it is arbitrary and uncertain. According to Muslims, all who reject Islam are doomed. Holy efforts to spread Islam by ridding the world of "infidels" are called "jihad." Much brutality has resulted from jihad. The five pillars of this false religion are (1) confession that Allah is the one true God and that Muhammed is his prophet, (2) prayer five times daily facing Mecca, (3) gifts of alms (money), (4) fasting during the month of Ramadan, and (5) making a pilgrimage to Mecca once during a lifetime. Islam oppresses much of the world. Women and those wanting to leave the faith especially face persecution.

Unlike Islam, Hinduism has no one founder. It began between 1800 and 1000 B.C. in India, and it teaches that everyone is part of God (Brahman) like drops in the sea. Devotees worship gods and goddesses which manifest Brahman. Many Hindus worship stone and wooden idols in temples. Hindus believe people are really God, but are unaware of it. Salvation is achieved via yoga and meditation, but requires many lifetimes of reincarnation into higher levels. Yoga involves meditation, chanting, postures, and breathing exercises. It produces an altered state of consciousness. If one has behaved well (good karma), he returns to life a little closer to union with Brahman. In other words, he may be a cow instead of an ant in the next life! No animals may be killed, for one may kill his mother if he ate a cow. This religion keeps India in poverty and squalor. If one has behaved badly, he is reborn to a lower life (bad karma) to pay for past sins by suffering. Hinduism is the foundation of the New Age Movement and transcendental meditation, which have become widely accepted in America by those who reject Jesus Christ.

Buddhism was founded in 525 B.C. in India as an offshoot of Hinduism. Buddhism is mostly atheistic. Some believe there is no God, while others speak of Buddha as a universal-enlightened consciousness or as a god. The goal is "nirvana," which is the elimination of all desires or cravings to escape suffering. Knowledge and good works lead one to nirvana. Buddhists believe there is no heaven or hell.

Judaism traces back to Abraham — about 2000 B.C. There are three separate branches of Judaism, each with its own beliefs. Orthodox Jews believe God is personal, all-powerful, eternal, and compassionate. Other Jews say He is impersonal and unknowable. Some Jews believe that prayer, repentance, and obeying the Law are necessary for salvation. Others think salvation means to improve society.

Biblical Christianity is not a religion. It is a personal relationship with a living Savior — Jesus Christ! The word "religion" means "to bind back" in Latin. It can refer to any system which binds men and women in legalistic bondage as they attempt to earn salvation by doing good works for God (Ephesians 2:8-9). Then men and women feel like they deserve credit, God's approval, and heaven. People readily compare themselves with others and find some reason to think they are better than their neighbors. They rationalize that God must accept them, thinking God "grades on a curve." But people who really know God are saved by faith in Jesus Christ alone. They know they deserve nothing but death and hell. They have no faith in their own efforts, their philosophy, or their religious works to save them. They rest in Christ's completed work of dying for them on the cross and they give Jesus Christ all the credit for their salvation. Liberty in the Spirit of God is the result. True salvation births neither a prohibitive legalism nor a license to live any way we please. Instead, we receive new desires and attitudes generated by the Holy Spirit in us. We grow to know God better each day.

Spiritual Sedation

Cold, dead religion is one of our worst enemies, for it inoculates us against a living, vital relationship with Jesus Christ. All of us have a deep, spiritual yearning for God, but religion consisting only of human works, mysterious feelings, empty rituals, or religious hype sedates us. Our real need is the person of Jesus Christ. Religion may take many different forms in keeping us sedated. Some formal meetings make God seem sterile and senile. Some informal meetings make Him seem like a "good ol' boy" to whom we can "buddy up" and put our arm around. Both present a false picture of God and they prevent us from really knowing Him.

Religion vs. Relationship

Religion leads to a false humility, as we try to think a little less of ourselves. Knowing God means not thinking of self at all, but focusing upon Jesus Christ! Religion means honoring God with only lip service. One who has a personal relationship with Jesus Christ honors Him with his or her heart and lips. Reading composed prayers in public to appear spiritual to others is a symptom of religion. Real prayer is crying out to God from the heart in the power of the Holy Spirit.

Religion puts Jesus in a secondary place, merely tacking His name onto the end of a prayer. One who knows Jesus understands that He is the "Door," the "Rock," the "Only Way," the "Truth," and the "Life." He is everything. The reality of the Holy Spirit must replace empty ritual. Holy ("Separate") living must replace hype. The authority of God's Word must replace humanity's denominational traditions so we can really know God. Inward reality must replace external appearance. Dead organization must be replaced by the living organism as believers function as a unit in Christ.

Religion means mankind using God to get what he or she wants. It is man demanding his way over God's way. A relationship with Jesus Christ means God works through us. In religion, people create God in their own image and seek their own self-made God. A relationship with Jesus means we acknowledge that God created us in His Image, sought us out, redeemed us from sin, and now lives within us.

Religion is self-improvement through self-reformation. Knowing Jesus, however, means death to selfish desires, a new identity in Jesus Christ, and life in the new nature He has given us. All human religions and cults involve human attempts to do something in hopes of being accepted by God and saved. Hinduism, Buddhism, Islam, Mormonism, Jehovah's Witnesses, and Unitarianism rely on a person's deeds to get him or her to Heaven. They all fail. Everyone who trusts in his or her own efforts is hopelessly lost. Jesus said, "I am the Way and the Truth and the Life. No one comes to the Father except through Me" (John 14:6).

Do you know Jesus Christ as your personal Savior? Is your hope based solely on Jesus Christ, the "Rock" of our salvation? Or do you have a cheap imitation, a religion that will leave you an eternal loser on judgment day?

RESCUE AND RECOVERY

THINKING IT THROUGH
    Who and what makes Christianity unique?
    Define "religion." Do you have "religion" or a relationship with Jesus Christ?
    How has your picture of God been faulty?

LISTENING TO GOD
    Ephesians 2:8-9

    John 14:6

    John 10:30

How does God's viewpoint change your thoughts and actions?

DIGGING OUT
Write out and pray the words of the tax collector in Luke 18:13:

Chapter 9
America: Before and After Judgment

ON APRIL 9, 2002, mountaineers Aaron Martin and Reid Sanders attempted to ski from the top of Alaska's 18,008-foot Mt. Elias, the second-highest peak in the United States. A climbing partner, John Griber, saw Martin slide several hundred feet and fall out of sight. Neither Sanders or Martin responded to calls. Griber was rescued by helicopter after carving "TWO DEAD" in huge letters in the snow. Two days later, a search team spotted two bodies in separate places above 16,000 feet. Presumed dead, the severe terrain made the recovery of their bodies unlikely.

Something as tragic as death in the snow and even more sinister has happened in our country. Americans have lost a reason for living beyond selfish gratification. We no longer serve a higher purpose. Many veteran educators notice signs in youth too big to miss. A sizable number of kids do not know what they want to become. College students and even many middle-aged people struggle with purpose and direction in life. Spiritually, we are "missing and presumed dead" in many parts of our culture.

Before the Slide
Before we turned away from God and the authority of His Word, America was a Christian nation. We were not Moslem, Hindu, or Buddhist. We were not neutral, and it is a fallacy to think any state can be neutral toward Christianity. God had a hand in our foundation, our laws, our constitution, and our system of governing. We were "one nation under God," though we were not perfect. Many people fell far short

55

of God's standards, for they permitted the evils of slavery. Many others trusted in God and we wrote it on our money. God blessed America. Even our tax laws reflected a Christian worldview. The state, knowing the land was God's, believed it had no right to tax land with a property tax. As John Adams wrote, "Our constitution was made only for a moral and religious people. It is wholly inadequate to the government of any other."[1] In colony after early colony, the stated purpose of our existence was the glory of God and the advancement of His kingdom. It was a requirement in some colonies for leadership to demonstrate saving faith in Jesus Christ and loyalty to God's Word as the authority of faith and practice. For example, the following oath of office was included in the constitution of the state of Delaware: "I do profess faith in God the Father, and in Jesus Christ His only Son, and in the Holy Ghost, one God, blessed for ever-more; I do acknowledge the Holy Scriptures of the Old and New Testaments to be given by divine inspiration."

Educational institutions were started to promote the knowledge of God and His Word. The purpose for Harvard College was plainly stated by its leaders: "Let every student be plainly instructed, and earnestly pressed to consider well, the main end of his life and studies is 'to know God and Jesus Christ which is eternal life (John 17:3) and therefore lay Christ in the bottom, as the only foundation of all sound knowledge and learning.'" Yale College was also based upon Biblical absolutes: "All scholars shall live religious, Godly and blameless lives according to the rules of God's Word, diligently reading the Holy Scriptures, the foundation of light and truth; and constantly attend upon all the duties of religion, both in public and secret." Most public schools were *Christian* schools and our early leaders governed from this perspective. William McGuffy's (1800-1873) reading books, written for the first six elementary grades, helped shape American education and morality for almost one hundred years. Over 120 million copies were sold. Below is a section from the 1837 *Eclectic Third Reader*. This is the material kids read when they learned to read:

> The Scriptures are especially designed to make us wise unto salvation through faith in Christ Jesus; to reveal to us the mercy of the Lord in Him; to form our minds after the likeness of God our Savior; to build up our souls in wisdom and faith, in love and holiness; to make us thoroughly furnished unto good works, enabling us to glorify God on earth; and, to lead us to an imperishable inheritance among the spirits of just men made perfect, and finally to be glorified with Christ in Heaven.

McGuffy was called "The Schoolmaster of the Nation." Yet, today's public schools would not use his historic works in training children to read because of their Christian content!

How Far Have We Fallen?

Eric Harris was one of the youthful Columbine killers in 1999. After his suicide, his body was discovered in a bloodstained, white T-shirt with the words "Natural Selection" on the front. His Web page listed many things he hated, but it also said this: "YOU KNOW WHAT I LOVE??? Natural SELECTION! . . . It's the best thing that ever happened to the Earth. Getting rid of all the stupid and weak organisms . . . but it's all natural! YES!"[2] Every school teacher who indoctrinates students with evolutionary belief should be shown Eric Harris' T-shirt. He carried out the logical conclusion of this agnostic belief system.

We have forsaken our Christian foundation. Leaders scoff at the fact that a sovereign, all-wise, all-powerful Creator made us for a purpose. When did rejection start? It started when we *rejected God's Word.* This rejection *preceded* interpretation of the "scientific" data! Darwin's theory made it appear that God was unnecessary. If things naturally developed, why bother with the supernatural? Thomas Huxley, Darwin's first disciple, invented the term "agnostic" to describe this indifference toward God. Agnostics do not claim that God does not exist, but only that we can have no knowledge of Him. So, they feel safe in ignoring the whole subject of God. Unfortunately, even many professing Christians have bought into the lie that things naturally develop. They have no idea how to defend the historic Christian faith because they do not study enough to know what the Scripture teaches! But if we are just evolved animals living by blind, random chance in a universe without moral accountability, why should we be surprised when our offspring live and act like animals? It is a miracle we do not have more Columbines!

Avalanche of National Judgment

Avalanches follow no rules. Prevention is the best survival tip. Unfortunately, it is too late for America to avoid judgment. We have turned against God and are already under judgment for our national sins. Thousands of churches are apostate (fallen away) and do not even know it! They "celebrate diversity" by inviting all forms of false religions (Islam, Hinduism, New Agers, and religious science groups) into joint prayer services. It is no wonder these churches have lost their influence for God! Too many individuals reject the revelation God gave of Himself in Jesus Christ. Our laws have been changed to prohibit prayer in schools, Christian symbols on public property, and God's commandments in our courtrooms. Tolerance of Satan's lies has left us spiritually bankrupt. We have strayed far from God and allowed our medical doctors to kill forty-five million unborn babies in the womb since 1973, promoted lewdness in movies and on television, and tolerated sodomy, which used to be illegal. Many now call evil "good" and good "evil."

Historically, when people exchanged God's truths for lies, He gave them over to homosexuality and terrible diseases, the "due penalty for their perversion" (Romans 1:25-27). Commentator William Barclay says there can be little doubt that homosexuality was one of the main causes of the final collapse of the Roman civilization. When ancient nations left God, He turned humanity against itself, and rampant vice resulted (Zechariah 8:10). Bad laws replaced good laws that were disobeyed (Ezekiel 20:24-25) and lawsuits "sprang up like poisonous weeds" to strangle the judicial system" (Hosea 10:4). Men of courage were replaced by the weak, inexperienced, and unqualified who turned Israel away when God's people forsook His ways (Isaiah 3). Injustice reigns in courts when a nation falls into wickedness, for God blindfolds the judges (Job 9:24)!

Could it be that September 11, 2001, was a wake-up call to America? Will God give America over to her enemies? He is calling America to repent of her sins and to forsake them. How long will we delay to repent? After a few stunning days, many leaders called for a return to "normal" living. Like ancient Israel (Isaiah 9:9-13), our pride was wounded. Some soon vowed to rebuild. But we must determine to *repent!* What has become "normal" is the most likely reason for our catastrophes! On national television, commentator Bryant Gumbel asked, "Why didn't God stop this or do something about this (disaster)?" Ann Graham Lotz replied, "For years, we have told God we didn't want Him in our schools. We didn't want Him in our government and we didn't want Him in our finances and God was being a perfect Gentleman in doing just what we asked Him to do. We need to make up our minds. Do we want God or do we not want Him? We cannot just ask Him in when disaster strikes."

RESCUE AND RECOVERY

How do you know America was a Christian nation? Do you think September 11, 2001, was a wake-up call for America?

Why do you think John Adams said our constitution would only work for people who were "moral and religious"?

Discuss the difference between an "atheist" and an "agnostic."

LISTENING TO GOD
Isaiah 3

Isaiah 9:8-16

Ezekiel 20:24-25

How does God's viewpoint change your thoughts and actions?

DIGGING OUT
Write out and pray the words of Psalm 51:10:

SECTION II

LIGHT AND HOPE

Chapter 10
Light at the End of the Tunnel

WHEN A PERSON is out of the light for an extended period of time, he or she may actually become physically blind. Those who have avoided or denied the light today are spiritually blind! We would not even know what God is like unless He revealed Himself to us. What is God like? Many folks picture God as an old man with a long, white beard who must lean on a cane. He is rather likable, but senile. Maybe He used to have some power a long time ago, but, for them, He is inept at solving modern problems. Nothing could be further from the truth.

God is completely self-sufficient. He has always existed and He needs no one to continue to exist and to thrive as God. We cannot comprehend His infinite existence because our minds are finite. Yet, we can trust Him. He is entirely trustworthy and He rewards those who diligently seek Him (Hebrews 11:6).

God is a Spirit. It is disrespectful to speak of Him as "the man upstairs." He is not restricted by time, location, or space. He is everywhere all the time! Yet, He is personal. He speaks. Most of the time, He speaks through His Word by His Spirit. As stated earlier, He speaks through His creation. He has emotions of anger (Judges 10:7), grief (Ephesians 4:30), wrath (Romans 1:18), hatred (Psalm 5:5), compassion (Psalm 103), and joy (Isaiah 62:5). These emotions are not "mixed emotions." They contain no human imperfections. He has every right to be angry when His people seek false gods. He hates sin for what it does to us. God has a will. He is purposeful. He plans ahead and He is not a quitter!

God is a Trinity. He is Father, Son, and Holy Spirit. All are co-equal and eternal. He is three-in-one. We see the Trinity in Christ's baptism (Matthew 3:13-17), His resurrection (Luke 24), the creation (Colossians 1:16-18), and the inspiration of Scripture (II Peter 1:20-21). We cannot fathom the Trinity. As someone has said, "Try to explain the Trinity and you'll lose your mind; but try to deny it, and you'll lose your soul."

God knows everything about everything! *We* gain a little wisdom and knowledge by experience. *God* has all wisdom and knowledge by His very essence!

God is all-powerful. He can do whatever He pleases and whatever is consistent with His perfect nature. He created all things out of nothing (Hebrews 11:3), with a spoken word (Psalm 33:6-9) by the Lord Jesus Christ (Colossians 1:15-17). But, God cannot lie, for that is inconsistent with His nature. He controls and preserves creation and, yet, He judges His creation.

Furthermore, God never changes. He is consistent. He is sovereign, which means He causes or allows everything to happen that does happen. He prevents other things from happening. He is consistently working out His eternal plan.

God is truth. Whatever He says is true. Whatever He predicts will come to pass. Whatever He says is false is false. Whatever He promises to do, He will do because He is truth.

God is love. Love is manifested in action. His love is revealed in Jesus Christ, who became man and died for us, His created beings. He constantly reaches out to us in love. In so doing, God is merciful, for we certainly do not deserve His love. Jesus healed blind, lame, and sick people. He still does so today. He also saves sinners who repent.

God is holy. He is without any spot of sin. He is light; "in him there is no darkness at all" (I John 1:5). He cannot tolerate wrong, nor can He be tempted by evil. He is completely set apart from sin. His holiness is expressed in His righteousness. He is always right, and whenever we disagree with Him in word or deed, we are wrong!

Because God is just, He must punish sin. He is the "Great Enforcer." We may think we get away with sin, but we never do. There are always consequences of our sin. Yet, God is patient. He is slow to get angry. He is graceful in patience. He is faithful to all who call upon Him. His "faithfulness reaches to the skies" (Psalm 57:10).

Finally, He is glorious! His glory is awesome. If we were to enter His presence, we would be compelled to fall on our faces in humble worship of our Creator. He is "God Almighty," the "Everlasting God" who provides, heals, leads, and fights for those who love Him!

God is the ultimate source of light in the world. We have exchanged the truth of God for a lie! Our sin has covered us in an avalanche of darkness as devastating as the ice blocks that engulfed the Phelps brothers. We cannot see God because of that sin. Yet, He continually reaches out to us in His great love. God's grace is quick to rescue everyone who turns from sin and runs into His powerful arms!

RESCUE AND RECOVERY

THINKING IT THROUGH

How would you respond to someone who says you cannot really know God or what He is like?

How does God speak to people?

Does God always punish sin immediately? Does He ever punish sin immediately? When has He done so?

LISTENING TO GOD

Colossians 1:16-18

John 1:1-5

I Peter 1:24-25

How does God's viewpoint change your thoughts and actions?

DIGGING OUT

Write out and pray the words of Psalm 57:9-11:

Chapter 11
The Clearly Marked Trail

SINCE SIR EDMUND HILLARY and Sherpa Tenzing Norgay first scaled Mt. Everest on May 29, 1953, climbing teams have tried to reach the summit of the world's tallest peak each spring. Some 800 people have succeeded, but authorities say 181 others have died on the unpredictable slopes.

There are fourteen known ways to approach the 29,035-foot mountain, with the uncharted East Ridge from Nepal being the only one never successfully conquered. It is called the "Fantasy Route." The territory is unknown. The rock face is almost vertical. Nails must be hammered into the mountain and ropes used to open a path. Temperatures at a Tibetan base camp 11,000 feet below the peak reach four below zero! Loose rocks dangerously balance on each side of the trail and avalanches fall frequently. Yawning crevices require the use of bulky ladders. Stone ledges are too narrow for mountaineers to set up temporary shelters for the night. It would be rare, in fact unparalleled, for any team to succeed via the East Ridge.

God has not left such an a impossible trail to discover His nature and His marvelous plan of salvation. He has clearly marked out the path for us in His Word. He is worthy of knowing and no one need miss Him!

The Bible is reliable. It claims to be the Word of God (II Timothy 3:16). Over 2,000 times, the Bible says, "Thus says the Lord," "God said," or "the Lord spoke."

As far as we know, no original manuscripts of Scripture exist today. If they existed, many people would probably worship them as religious relics. But, compared to other historical writings, there is more evidence to believe in the authenticity of the New Testament than for almost any ten pieces of classical literature combined! If we believe any piece of literature, we have more reason to believe the Bible. Note the following chart comparing the work, when it was written, the earliest copies available, the span of time between the original manuscript and the current available manuscript, and the number of copies we have found:

Work	Date Original Was Written	Earliest Copy Found	Time Between Original and Earliest Known Copy	Number of Manuscripts in Existence
New Testament	45-100 A.D.	C. 325 A.D, (Parts in 130 A.D.)	50-500 years	24,970
Caesar's Wars	100-44 B.C	900 A.D.	1,000 years	10
Plato	400 B.C.	900 A.D.	1,300 years	7
Aristotle	384-322 B.C.	1100 A.D.	1,400 years	5
Herodotus (History)	480-425 B.C.	900 A.D.	1,350 years	8

Objective evidence for the authenticity of Scripture is overwhelming.

The Scriptures are consistent. The sixty-six books of the Bible were written over 1,500 years by forty different authors in three languages on three continents. Yet, there are no contradictions! Only forty lines out of 20,000 are even debatable today. If you perceive a contradiction between two passages, either you misunderstand one or the other or both! Nearly every major heresy begins with a misreading of the Biblical text. Here are some examples of what people say about Scripture and what Scripture really says:

"Money is the root of all evil" is a favorite saying of man. The Bible says, "The *love* of money is a root of all kinds of evil" (I Timothy 6:10).

Some people say, "Jesus never claimed to be God." However, John 5:18 records that ". . .(Jesus) was even calling God His own Father, making Himself equal with God." John 10:30 quotes Jesus as saying, "I and the Father are one." His claim is unique among recognized religious leaders. Neither Mohammed nor Confucius nor Ghandi nor Buddha claimed to be God. Jesus did claim to be God and the *only* way to heaven. Either He was a liar, a lunatic, or He is Lord of all!

Some people say, "Jesus was just a great moral teacher." But Scripture has not left us this option. John 20:31 says, "But these have been written that you may believe that Jesus is the Christ, the Son of God. . . ."

Some people say, "We are all gods or part of God." The Bible says, ". . .the Lord is God; besides Him there is no other" (Deuteronomy 4:35). Isaiah 44:8 asks, ". . .Is there any God besides Me? No, there is no other Rock; I know not one."

Some people say, "All religions lead to the same end. No one religion is right." The Bible says, "Salvation is found in no one else" (Acts 4:12).

Others say, "We are reincarnated from a past life and we will be reincarnated in a future life." The Bible says God created Adam from dust, Eve came from Adam's rib and all people came from them (Genesis 2). Furthermore, people die once, and then comes judgment (Hebrews 9:27).

The writers of Scripture were credible eyewitnesses (II Peter 1:16, I John 1:3, Acts 2:22). Their lives were changed by what they saw and heard. They went from doubters to self-sacrificing servants willing to die for the Christ they had followed and had seen risen from the dead.

Archaeology confirms the Scripture. In his book, *Rivers in the Desert,* Dr. Nelson Glueck, a famous Jewish archaeologist, said, "It may be stated categorically that no archaeological discovery has ever controverted a Biblical reference."

Fulfilled prophecy confirms the authenticity of Scripture. Jesus fulfilled over sixty major Old Testament prophecies and approximately 270 ramifications alone! He was born in Bethlehem as predicted (Micah 5:2, Matthew 2:1). John the Baptist prepared the way for Him (Malachi 3:1, Matthew 3:1). He entered Jerusalem on a colt (Zechariah 9:9, Matthew 21:6-11). He was betrayed by a friend (Zechariah 13:5, Matthew 26:49-50) for thirty pieces of silver (Zechariah 11:12, Matthew 27:5-7). He was innocent, yet made no self-defense (Isaiah 53:7, Matthew 27:14-19). He was crucified (Psalm 22:16, Matthew 27:35). None of His bones were broken (Psalm 34:20, John 19:33). The reaction of the crowd was predicted (Isaiah 50:6, Matthew 27:67). He was given gall and vinegar (Psalm 69:21, Matthew 27:34). The details of His burial were predicted (Isaiah 53:9, Matthew 27:57-60).

Furthermore, twenty different non-Christian sources record sixty to sixty-five facts concerning the life of Jesus.

The Bible holds universal appeal to people and has changed the lives of readers. It has endured the test of time, despite being attacked and vilified more than any other book. English scholar John Wycliffe drew so much anger for advocating a Bible in English that church officials dug up his bones and burned them about forty years after his death in 1384. William Tyndale was condemned for translating the Bible into English. He was strangled to death and his body was burned in 1536 in England. The list of martyrs who have died for their faith is almost endless and it is growing daily by leaps and bounds.

Voltaire, the French infidel who died in 1778, said that in 100 years from his time, Christianity would be swept from existence and passed into history. What happened? Only fifty years after his death, the Geneva Bible Society used his printing press and house to produce stacks of Bibles!

God's trail to eternity is clearly marked. His way of salvation is based upon trust in the Lord Jesus Christ as personal Savior. People miss God's trail only because they want to miss it!

RESCUE AND RECOVERY

THINKING IT THROUGH

What would you say to someone who says the Bible cannot be trusted?

How do most major heresies begin?

Describe your feelings if a teacher or friend called you bigoted or intolerant for insisting Jesus is God and the only way to God.

LISTENING TO GOD

Acts 2:22

Acts 4:12

John 20:31

How does God's viewpoint change your thoughts and actions?

DIGGING OUT

Write out and pray the words of Matthew 11:25:

Chapter 12
Avalanche Avoidance

LONG BEFORE HILLARY AND NORGAY returned from Mt. Everest in 1953, George Mallory had obtained permission from the Dalai Lama to try the climb in 1921. Over a three-year period, Mallory and his party made three attempts. When asked why he wanted to climb Mt. Everest, Mallory replied, "Because it is there."

Mallory's ambition proved to be fatal. He and his climbing partner, Andrew Irvine, persisted on the North slope in 1924. It was not until seventy-five years later that his body was positively identified and buried, but whether Mallory and Irvine reached the summit twenty-nine years before Hillary and Norgay remains the greatest mystery in mountaineering. Did Mallory die in an avalanche? Whatever the cause of death, his ambition was both a blessing and a trap!

Ambition to read God's Word is a blessing, but if we hope to avoid the "avalanche traps" of life, we must understand it! Mishandling Scripture through ignorance or outright unbelief has a snowball effect that results in disaster on life's slippery slopes.

Though understanding Scripture can be difficult, it is well worth the effort! The goal is to discover exactly what God says in His Word so we can obey it. The process of inductive Bible study involves three steps. They are (1) observation, (2) interpretation, and (2) application. The next three chapters discuss these three steps.

OBSERVATION

To reduce the risk of avalanche in the high country, it is vital to identify avalanche terrain. Avalanches run repeatedly year after year in the same areas. The slopes are called "avalanche paths." These are most often slopes of thirty to forty-five degrees, but they sometimes start on slopes as shallow as twenty-five degrees.

To identify avalanche terrain in life, we must understand God's Word. Understanding God's Word begins with *reading* it. It is amazing how many people will argue that God's Word is irrelevant when they have never read it! We must read and think about what is actually stated in the text. A daily, personal "quiet time" with God and His Word is essential. Jesus got alone with God early in the morning (Mark 1:35). His was a good pattern to follow, for most people are much more alert in the morning than late at night. Pray for God to reveal His truth to you. Devotional commentaries can be helpful.

Inerrancy and Inspiration

Remember, every word of Scripture in inerrant and inspired (Psalm 119:130, 160; I Corinthians 2:13; Revelation 22:18-19). Scripture is therefore authoritative over our experiences, traditions, and opinions. II Timothy 3:16-17 says all Scripture is inspired by God. God "breathed" out the Scriptures and used the personalities of the human authors to express His perfect revelation to man. Peter wrote that men moved by the Holy Spirit spoke from God (II Peter 1:21). God's Word did not come from man. "Above all, you must understand that no prophecy of Scripture came about by the prophet's own interpretation" (II Peter 1:20). *Moved* is the word used to describe a sailboat moving under the power of a strong wind. The "wind" of God is the Holy Spirit. Scripture is inerrant. The original manuscripts had no errors whatsoever and there have been surprisingly few errors in transmission over the years. God has supernaturally preserved His Word for us to believe and obey.

Truth Is Revealed by God

Alex Lowe was the biggest name in the ego-building sport of mountaineering. His strength, speed, and courage made him seem invulnerable. Twice he climbed to the summit of Mt. Everest. His assistance in daring rescues of stranded mountain climbers made him a hero. But on October 4, 1999, Lowe and cameraman Dave Bridges were engulfed in a 500-foot-wide, 100-mile-per-hour avalanche in the Tibetan Himalayas. Trying to become the first to ski from the summit of Mt. Shishapangma, the world's 14th-highest peak, Lowe lost his life. His death was stunning. As Dr. Colin Grissom stated, "He was the one who could push the limits and live."

Not this time.

Truth is revealed by God and not figured out by humans. Just as Alex Lowe was not invincible on top of a mountain, no one is sufficient within himself or herself to figure out either God or His Word! The things of God are "foolishness" to anyone who will not trust Him (I Corinthians 2:14). No person today has insights that no one else has ever been given. We must willingly submit to Biblical authority and the leading of the Holy Spirit. The Spirit never contradicts the Word of God. Ask God to reveal the truth to you and He will do it.

Revelation over Time

Thousands of skiers, climbers, and snowmobilers have triggered avalanches and lived to tell about it. After all, for every fifteen people caught in an avalanche, fourteen will escape and only one will die. Rescue gear is essential. A small shovel and a beacon light are two invaluable items in a snowfield. Most avalanche victims cannot survive a burial of thirty minutes or longer, and beacons and shovels are the best ways to recover. Escape takes time. Be patient.

God has revealed Himself over time from the Old Testament to the New Testament. His nature becomes increasingly clear as we read through Scripture. Use the Old Testament to interpret the New Testament (Hebrews 7). Old Testament stories do not teach doctrines, but they do illustrate them! Both testaments are valuable tools in digging for meaning.

Observation is the first step to understanding God's Word. Time spent reading and meditating upon God's Word is time well spent.

RESCUE AND RECOVERY

THINKING IT THROUGH

What are the three steps to understanding God's Word?

Who makes God's Word clear to us? Why do people who do not trust God not understand the Bible?

Whom do you know who accepts the authority of Scripture over their opinions, traditions, and religious experiences?

LISTENING TO GOD

II Timothy 3:16-17

II Peter 1:20-21

II Corinthians 5:7

How does God's viewpoint change your thoughts and actions?

DIGGING OUT

Write out and pray the words of Psalm 119:33-34:

Chapter 13
Monster Slides

THE HIGHLAND BOWL, a stupendous amphitheater formed by the north and south ridges of Highlands Peak near Aspen, Colorado, is the site of hundreds of avalanches each winter. During heavy winters, monster slides roar almost a vertical mile to the valley floor. Mountaineers who successfully climb there become complacent. Those who lose their fear have no judgment. They become vulnerable.

INTERPRETATION

In preventing life's "monstrous slides," we must correctly *interpret* Scripture (II Timothy 2:15). We are to "correctly handle" the word of truth. Misinterpretation is "avalanche terrain." We must ask ourselves "What *does* the Scripture mean?" not "What do I *want* it to mean?" Several principles help our understanding of the meaning of the passage under consideration:

Literal Meaning

A student who holds no respect for Scripture and hastily spiritualizes it becomes vulnerable to misinterpretation. When the plain sense makes sense, seek no other sense! Do not spiritualize or allegorize Scripture unless the text itself requires it. Scripture is figurative when it says it is figurative or when the literal is impossible, absurd, or contradictory to the clear teaching of other Scripture. For example, Jesus does not want us to maim ourselves (Matthew 5:29-30), but He is very serious about sin. We do not produce literal fruit on our bodies, but we are to bear spiritual fruit (John 15:16). Often, if

Scripture is figurative, it tells us so (Hebrews 11:19, Galatians 4:24). A good rule of thumb when studying any Scripture is found in the golden rule of Biblical interpretation, as stated by Dr. David L. Cooper: "When the plain sense of Scripture makes common sense, seek no other sense, but take every word at its primary, literal meaning unless the facts of the immediate context clearly indicate otherwise."

The Meaning Is in the Text

Sometimes the snow shows clear and present danger signs of an avalanche. The best clue is fresh avalanches. Snow that collapses beneath one's feet or sends cracks shooting ahead are also danger signs. More than one inch of snow per hour or strong winds blowing snow plumes off the ridges signal danger. Hikers must carefully observe and evaluate.

Likewise, we must carefully observe and evaluate every word of Scripture. The meaning of the text is in the text, not in man's subjective (often mystic) response to it. We must use the natural, usual sense of words and grammar in the original writing to determine meaning. Paying attention to syntax (how the words relate to each other) is vital in reading signs and determining meaning.

One Interpretation

Following an old track on a mountain does not mean a slope is safe. Such an assumption is presumption. Presumption has led to disaster both on the slopes and in study of Scripture. Great leaders of the past (Augustine, Luther, Calvin, Wesley, etc.) are sometimes helpful, but they were not correct about everything just because they were great leaders! None of them had it all together. Yet, all had the correct interpretation of many passages. The Holy Spirit is needed to understand the meaning (I Corinthians 2:11-15).

There is *one interpretation,* but there are *many appli-cations* of the truth. Do not presume an alternative meaning is valid because someone thinks it is a good idea! Base applications upon the interpretation, not interpretation upon an application.

For You, But Not *to* You

Mountaineers who have huge egos and are impa-tient will sooner or later make a mistake. In addition, all risk sports give one feelings of invincibility. These feelings are imaginary and have nothing to do with snow moving at 100 miles per hour. More than 100 years ago, Edward Whymper confronted these feel-ings during his first ascent of the Matterhorn. "A momentary negligence may destroy the happiness of a lifetime," he wrote after four of his companions fell to their deaths on that famous climb.

Egotism when it comes to interpreting Scripture is also dangerous. We must not be so egotistical as to think that all Scripture is written to us. It is vital to determine to whom the author was writing. The mean-ing can be totally lost if we do not understand this principle. However, all Scripture is of value to us. It is written *for* us and we can derive value from it, whether or not it was addressed *to* us!

Silence

Like avalanche education, studying Scripture is "hard by the yard, but a cinch by the inch." We can-not understand everything all at once. It is a lifelong endeavor. Scripture does not speak on every subject. All is not yet revealed by our God. We do not know it all! Where Scripture is silent, we should remain si-lent, but where it speaks, we can speak confidently.

Bad Behavior

Attitudes can get us in trouble. We can be so goal-oriented in climbing a certain peak or skiing a certain area that we take unwarranted risks. Sometimes we can be so close to reaching a goal that we overlook danger signs. Group dynamics or peer pressure cloud good judgment. Haste and fatigue cloud decision-making.

The Bible is honest in recording the bad decisions of some of its most famous characters. King David was guilty of adultery and murder and paid dearly for his sins for the rest of his life. So does anyone else who sins as he did. Do not think you can sin and get away with it simply because it is recorded that some of God's choice servants fell. Nobody gets away with sin. The final hero of all stories in Scripture is God!

Picturing the Truth

One does not have to die in an avalanche or be so scared that he or she wishes to be dead to have "avalanche savvy." But we do need to work at learning about snow and avalanches before we can have valid confidence to make a "go or do not go" decision.

A person with savvy in God's Word recognizes there are "types" (examples) in the Old Testament that picture New Testament truth (I Corinthians 10:11). For example, Isaac is a "type" of Christ. Isaac willingly allowed his father, Abraham, to tie him to an altar, offering himself as a sacrifice (Genesis 22). But God did not require Abraham to kill Isaac. He provided a substitute, a ram caught in the thicket, to complete the picture. In this sense, the ram is also representative of Jesus Christ, who died in our place. With experience, one can readily identify pictures of New Testament truth. Sermon notes and Bible commentaries can help.

Context

Digging snow pits and performing stress tests on a test slope near the slope you want to ski can reveal the danger of an avalanche. A hole several feet wide and four to five feet deep can reveal changes in layering, texture, and strength. On a small slope or at the edge of a large slope, jump on your skis or do a quick ski cut in a transverse direction to see if the snow fractures. Also, from above a steep slope, kick off a block of ice the size of a person and let it fall. This test simulates the weight of one or more skiers on the slope without putting anyone at risk.

The test of context is always essential when studying Scripture. A text cannot mean what it never could have meant to its author or to its original readers! Find out as much as possible about the geographical area and the people to whom the book was written. Commentaries and Bible dictionaries can help. We must interpret according to the context of the passage to get the flow of the argument. We must also interpret according to the context of the book. What did the writer mean when he used the word elsewhere? Obscure passages yield to clear passages. Finally, we must interpret according to the context of the entire Bible, for Scripture never contradicts itself. A text without a context is a pretext!

Study with a Method

On March 31, 1984, Chris Kessler, Craig Soddy, and Tom Snyder were doing avalanche control work in Highland Bowl in Colorado. The three ski patrollers set off explosives near the top of the Bowl. Their bombs showed no sign of danger. With tragic false confidence, they skied closer to the middle of the Bowl and into the midst of a vast avalanche path. They exploded three more charges. The second explosion triggered a slide below them. Then suddenly, a gigantic avalanche fell on them from above. All three men died.

Kessler, Soddy, and Snyder were not as methodical as they should have been in their efforts to control an avalanche. We *must* be methodical as we study Scripture. We must not assume we can know everything by studying fragments of Scripture here and there. Study a book at a time. Discover the author's purpose in writing. The Scriptures were written in books or letters, not separate passages. Studying a book or letter keeps us from taking passages out of context. There are books of history, poetry, law, prophecy, and instruction. Prophecy, for example, almost always has both immediate and long-term applications. The book of Acts reveals the history of the Church and was not written to teach doctrine. Christians differ on minor issues such as how to select leaders, the frequency of communion, and mode of baptism. These things ought not to divide. As someone said long ago, let us have "unity in essentials, liberty in nonessentials, and charity in everything!"

Limited Understanding

Sometimes a combination of conditions can cause an avalanche. Snow is most unstable during and after snowfalls or after prolonged heating by the sun, especially on steep inclines. The most dangerous avalanches usually occur on convex slopes. Also, snow crystals in the shape of needles and pellets result in more unstable snow conditions than star-shaped snowflakes. We do not understand all possible varieties of conditions.

Similarly, Old Testament prophets did not understand all they predicted (I Peter 1:10-12). For that matter, neither did some New Testament prophets. As time goes on, their accuracy was and is being remarkably confirmed! Sometimes our understanding must wait for God's perfect timing.

85

Culture

One can always walk or ski safely on slopes up to twenty-five degrees and ninety-five percent of the time on slopes up to thirty degrees. An inexpensive slope meter is valuable. However, be cautious when steeper slopes lie above you: it is still possible to trigger avalanches on slopes far above you.

By understanding the "slopes" of the cultural context, it is possible to discover what a text meant to the people in the day in which it was written and, therefore, the meaning. As previously stated, a text cannot mean today what it did not mean to the original audience. Some texts apply strictly to the culture or situation in which they were written. Examples include commands to greet one another with a holy kiss (I Corinthians 16:20), prohibitions against food offered to idols (I Corinthians 10:23-29), use of wine as medicine (I Timothy 5:23), and Paul's preference for singleness in light of the current persecution (I Corinthians 7). Other texts list practices that remain wrong in every time and culture. Examples include adultery, idolatry, drunkenness, homosexuality, stealing, and greed (I Corinthians 6:9-10).

Principles or Commands?

There is a difference between avalanche principles and commands. One principle is that south-facing slopes are more dangerous in the spring. An example of a command is that one should never take *any* slope for granted.

In the Bible, there are general principles (which can have exceptions) and specific commands (which allow for no exceptions). Many Proverbs are general principles. The commands of the law are specific and without exception.

Original Language

Sun crust on old snow can cause new snow to slide off. Test and retest the snow!

We must carefully test each new translation to be sure it is true to the best manuscripts. New, twisted translations can be as unstable as new snow!

The original language has priority over translations in determining the meaning. Test the Scripture by finding out what was meant in the original. Again, some Bible commentaries can provide great help.

RESCUE AND RECOVERY

THINKING IT THROUGH

"An ounce of prevention is worth a pound of cure." How does this statement apply to interpreting God's Word?

Do you have a daily, personal quiet time with God and His Word? How might it change your words, thoughts, and actions?

What is the difference between interpretation and application of Scripture?

LISTENING TO GOD

II Timothy 2:15

Romans 15:4

I Corinthians 10:11

How does God's viewpoint change your thoughts and actions?

DIGGING OUT

Write out and pray the words of Psalm 138:1-3:

Chapter 14
Overcoming Blindness

SNOW BLINDNESS is an alarming condition. It is caused by bright sunshine or snow or light-colored rock. The eyes become bloodshot and feel irritated and full of sand. Thankfully, it is not permanent. Cool, wet compresses, two pairs of sunglasses, and aspirin usually restore sight in two or three days.

Spiritual blindness is even worse than snow blindness. The first step in restoring spiritual sight is reading God's Word (observation). The second step is understanding it (interpretation). The final step in restoring spiritual sight is to apply what we have observed in God's Word and interpreted as God's will. The first two steps are futile without the third!

APPLICATION

Jesus promised happiness to His children if we *do* what He has taught us (John 13:17). Indeed, those who have true faith in the Lord Jesus apply His Word to their lives and *do* it (John 8:39, 14:15, 23, 15:14). James tells us not to merely listen to the Word, but to *do* what it says (James 1:22). If we only listen, we are self-deceived. But if actions follow, we will be blessed (happy, fortunate). The blessing is in the doing!

Ask yourself, "What does Scripture tell me to do?" not "What do I want it to mean?" Apply the truth of God's Word to your life. Do not read the Bible casually or take it for granted. Beware of knowledge without action and of indifference to conviction!

Words have definite meaning. God's Word is especially to be taken seriously. We are warned never to add to or take away from His Word (Revelation 22:18-19). His Word is a lamp to our feet and a light to our path (Psalm 119:105). It is eternal, standing firm in the heavens (Psalm 119:89). God's Word is understandable to His children. We are wise to read, study, and obey it! It is the only way to overcome spiritual blindness!

Power to See, Understand, and Act

Spiritual insight is restored only by the illumination of the Holy Spirit. That is why an unbeliever in Jesus Christ (God's living Word) will never understand God's written Word. He has been spiritually blinded by his own unbelief. Many Americans are deceived into believing that all points of view are equally valid. These people are self-deceived because they reject God's Word as authoritative. They are deceived by Satan, who deceives all who reject the God of the Bible (II Corinthians 4:4; Revelation 12:9, 20:3). Almighty God allows them to be deceived because they have rejected His truth and believed a lie (II Thessalonians 2:9-11).

When a person really believes God, he rests all beliefs and values upon the foundation of God's Word. God gives His Holy Spirit to such a person, who can then accurately interpret Scripture. I Corinthians 2:10-16 says:

> The Spirit searches all things, even the deep things of God. For who among men knows the thoughts of a man except the man's spirit within him? In the same way, no one knows the thoughts of God except the Spirit of God. We have not received the spirit of the world but the Spirit who is from God, that we may understand what God has freely given us. This is what we speak, not in words taught us by human wisdom but in words taught by the Spirit, expressing spiritual truths in spiritual words. The man without the Spirit does not accept the things that come from the Spirit of God, for they are foolishness to him, and he cannot understand them, because they are spiritually discerned. The spiritual man makes judgments about all things, but he himself is not subject to any man's judgment: For who has known the mind of the Lord that he may instruct him? But we have the mind of Christ.

We know the truths of Scripture because the Holy Spirit teaches us! Truth is not figured out by man's intellect. Truth is revealed by God's Spirit to those who believe God! Satan has erected strongholds (evolution, atheism, humanism) against the knowledge of God. Only God's power demolishes these arguments and pretensions that keep men from Him (II Corinthians 10:4-6).

Similarly, one who refuses to believe God's Word can not please God in word or deed. Man's unbelief cuts off the power to live a Christ-like life like pulling a plug from a socket cuts off electrical power. We depend upon the Holy Spirit to see truth, interpret truth, and act upon truth.

Is belief in God's Word the majority view? Not today! But truth does not depend upon majority vote! God has established His Word independent of the numbers of people who believe it. At one time, the entire world except for eight people disbelieved God and perished in Noah's flood. In Lot's day, he was the *only* righteous man in the city of Sodom. God rescued him before raining fire and brimstone upon all the ungodly (Luke 17:26-36). Jesus indicated that the time before His return would be marked by persecution, apostasy, and unbelief (Matthew 24:9-13, 24). Persistent, abiding faith in the true and living God will be rare (Luke 18:8). We must be very near His return!

RESCUE AND RECOVERY

THINKING IT THROUGH

What does God promise to those who do what He has told them?

What have those who only listen to God's Word done to themselves?

In what areas do you know what God wants you to do, but, so far, you have not obeyed?

LISTENING TO GOD

James 1:22-25

John 13:17

John 15:14

How does God's viewpoint change your thoughts and actions?

DIGGING OUT

Write out and pray the words of Psalm 141:3-4:

Chapter 15
The Only Eyewitness

JUST AS WE DO NOT KNOW everything about avalanches, we do not know everything about the past. But we do know many things upon which to base our lives and our conduct. And we know them because God, the only One present when the past took place, has given us a written record!

First, we know that God created everything out of nothing ("bara") in six days ("yom"). "Bara" means "out of nothing." Humans cannot create anything out of nothing. "Bara" is only used in Scripture with God as the subject. "Yom" is equally precise. It is used approximately 410 times outside Genesis 1. Each use of this Hebrew word for "day" in the Old Testament, when preceded by a number, means "an ordinary day." We conclude the same is true in Genesis. As defined by God, the light is called "Day" (Genesis 1:5). One evening and one morning constituted one night and one day (Genesis 1:5, 8, 13, 19, 23, 31), the time required for one rotation of the earth on its axis. Following is the sequence God used, according to Scripture:

Day 1: At (Hebrew "bere'shith") the beginning, God created the heavens and the earth. He also said, "Let there be light." He provided light, He is light (John 1:5), and in eternity future, He will be the source of light (Revelation 21:23)! He separated the light from darkness, which made day and night (Genesis 1:5). It is probable that God had already created angels (Job 38:7). The earth was a vast ocean. It was "incomplete" and "empty." It was not "chaotic."

Day 2: God created the sky, giving the earth an atmosphere (Genesis 1:6-8). Water above the atmosphere was separated from water on earth.

Day 3: God gathered the earth's waters together, creating dry land (Genesis 1:9-10). He drew the limits for the shore lines (Job 38:4-11) and He created plants, trees, and other vegetation (Genesis 1:11-13). The earth took shape like clay under a seal (Job 38:14).

Day 4: God created the sun, moon, and stars (Genesis 1:14-19). They are light-bearers and the means for establishing a calendar to measure time. He determined the number of the stars and called them by name (Psalm 147:4).

Day 5: God created fish and birds (Genesis 1:20-23).

Day 6: God created land animals (including dinosaurs, though the word would not be coined until 1841), man, and woman (Genesis 1:24-31). Man was made from dust, not from an animal (Genesis 2:7). Woman was made from man's rib. Human beings were —and are — the "crown" of His creation. We are made in God's likeness. Just as God is a Trinity, we are spirit, soul, and body. Just as God has intellect, a moral nature, the power to communicate, and an emotional nature, so do humans. We can communicate and design things. We are made by God to worship God! We were ordered to fill and subdue the earth and to rule God's creation. We were given great privilege and responsibility by God. God finished His creation and called it "very good."

Every person and every nation came from Adam (I Corinthians 15:45), who was created mature and functioning the moment he was created. Furthermore, God determined where and how long each person would live (Job 14:5; Acts 17:24-26). Adam, for example, lived for 930 years (Genesis 5:5)!

Every living thing in God's creation was complete and functioning the moment it was created. It was new and it was perfect. No improvement was necessary. Our lives have meaning only in relation to our Creator, who made us all (Isaiah 64:8; Psalm

119:73; Job 10:8). We may not understand every detail of God's creative genius, but we can rely upon His Word. He makes some details of creation very clear in Scripture, but it is through faith (not rationalistic thinking) that we understand that the universe was formed out of nothing at God's command (Hebrews 11:3). God, in His wisdom, saw to it that mankind would never find Him through our intellect or our human wisdom (I Corinthians 1:21).

> **Day 7:** God rested. He finished creation and it has been complete ever since (Hebrews 4:3). He blessed and sanctified this day. Moses recorded the truth as God inspired him. He wrote. "For in six days the Lord made the heavens and the earth, the sea, and all that is in them, but He rested on the seventh day" (Exodus 20:11). God did not have to rest. He was teaching us something very special (Exodus 31:15-17).

Secular historians puzzle over who invented the seven-day week. It does not exactly fit the 365 1/4 solar year or the twenty-nine-day moon month. Bible believing Christians know it came from God. But not everyone would receive God's teaching. This is understandable, for I Corinthians 2:14 tells us "The man without the Spirit does not accept the things that come from the Spirit of God, for they are foolishness to him, because they are spiritually discerned." For centuries, it was known and accepted by most scholars that Moses wrote the first five books of the Old Testament (Pentateuch). In the seventeenth century, a philosopher named Benedict Spinoza (1632-1677) questioned Moses' authorship. German seminaries of the 1800s produced a group which called itself the "Higher Critical School." They not only rejected Moses' authorship, but eventually rejected the historicity of the entire Bible, labeling much Scripture as "myth" or "legend".

Belief that God has no control over the world or people (deism) arose in the 1790s. Philosophies of Hegelian dialecticism ("Every thesis evokes its antithesis and the two unite in synthesis, so truth has therefore evolved.") and Darwinian evolution in the nineteenth century replaced the supernatural revelation of God in the minds of liberal intellectuals. The teachings of these unbelievers have thoroughly infiltrated many universities and seminaries in America today. Humans have become their own god, subjectively inventing their own "truth." For them, rationalism replaced revelation as a way to determine truth. But when people reject the Scriptures and the power of God, they descend into darkness (Matthew 22:24).

Bible-believing Christians are convinced that God supernaturally inspired the Pentateuch through Moses. Both the Old Testament (Exodus 17:14, 24:4, 34:27; Numbers 33:1-2; Deuteronomy 31:9; Joshua 1:7-8, 8:31-32; 1 Kings 2:3; 2 Kings 14:6, 21:8; Ezra 6:18; Nehemiah 13:1; Daniel 9:11-13; Malachi 4:4) and the New Testament (Matthew 19:8; Mark 12:26; John 1:45, 5:46-47; Acts 3:22; Romans 10:5) explicitly say so.

The Lord Jesus Christ said we must believe Moses. "'But do not think I will accuse you before the Father. Your accuser is Moses on whom your hopes are set. If you believed Moses, you would believe me, for he wrote about me. But if you do not believe what he wrote, how will you believe what I say? (John 5:45-47).

Second, Jesus was the Creator (Hebrews 1:2). He is the "Living Word of God" (John 1:3; Isaiah 44:24). All things were created by Jesus Christ and for Jesus Christ (Colossians 1:16). God created everything by His Word (II Peter 3:5-7). Psalm 33:6 and 9 says, "By the word of the LORD were the heavens made, their starry host by the breath of His mouth. For He spoke, and it came to be; He commanded, and it stood firm." Jesus believed the six-day creation account in Genesis (Mark 10:6; Matthew 19:4), which described the perfectly formed, mature bodies of Adam and Eve. He said, "But at the beginning of creation (not millions of years later) God 'made them male and female'" (Mark 10:6). Man's idea of evolution can not adequately explain the sexes. Man and woman were not primordial slime nor tadpoles before they were humans! Humans are not animals (I Corinthians 15:38-39). Therefore, humans must not live like animals. Humans are distinct from animals in that (1) they are made in God's likeness and (2) given dominion upon the earth (Psalm 8:6-8). Furthermore, humans are gifted by God with the ability to speak languages, to write, to create and invent, to record history, and to contemplate eternity (Ecclesiastes 3:11). Only humans pray, worship, bury their dead, and know right from wrong. Since humans are not even related to animals, no suitable companion was available for Adam before God created Eve.

Third, sin and death came into the world through Adam (Romans 5:12-21). Paul confirmed both the facts of Adam's and Eve's existence and of their sin (I Timothy 2:13-15). Therefore, there were no millions of years of death, decay, and struggle for survival before Adam's sin. God called His creation "good" and "very good." God finished creation and then subjected His creation to natural laws. But natural laws never create anything! Suffering, death, decay, and struggle for survival came as a result of Adam's sin. When man followed Satan, the enemy of our souls gained tremendous influence over man and the world (Ephesians 2:1-2). Only in Christ is man rescued (Colossians 1:13). If death did not originate with Adam, it follows that life does not come through Christ (I Corinthians 15:21-22).

Comprehensive genealogical records in Genesis 5, 10 and 11; I Chronicles; Matthew 1 and Luke 3 cover about 4,000 years of history from Genesis to Jesus' birth. The oldest known historical records of *any culture* are approximately 6,000 years old. The oldest coral reef in the world is 4,200 years old and the oldest tree is 4,600 years old. No one knows the exact age of the universe, but the overwhelming amount of true scientific evidence from earth and space limits earth's age to no more than about 10,000 years. Modern humanity has been sold a lie. One hundred fifty years ago, a few people who wanted to believe in evolution invented the "geological column," the ages (Anozoic, Mesozoic, etc.) and their preposterous dates. The worldwide flood of Noah, with its massive earthquakes, underwater volcanic eruptions, and sedimentary deposits, much better explains the evidence seen today. Whenever a textbook, college professor, or museum says earth is millions of years old, they are telling us we cannot trust God's Word. God created living things at a mature stage of life, for Adam and Eve were not babies! Radiometric dating methods have proven to be unreliable, often giving absurd ages to living or freshly killed specimens! They are based upon unprovable assumptions about both the original content of elements and their past decay rates. Yet, many humans have put faith in humanity's inconsistent and unreliable dating methods instead of the reliable Word of God!

Genesis 1 clearly states that the earth was created before the sun. In the so-called Big Bang Theory, the sun comes first. Therefore, we can reject the Big Bang Theory of creation on the basis of Scripture. There is a "big bang" coming at the *end,* however (II Peter 3:10)!

We can believe God, for He was the lone Eyewitness of His own creation! His Word is much more reliable than that of fallible mankind!

RESCUE AND RECOVERY

THINKING IT THROUGH

Why is it so difficult for those who do not know God to accept the fact that He created everything in six days?

What main facts would you use to try to help someone see the truth of God's creative schedule?

When and where did sin, suffering, and death originate?

LISTENING TO GOD

Exodus 20:11

Hebrews 11:3

I Corinthians 15:21-22

How does God's viewpoint change your thoughts and actions?

DIGGING OUT

Write out and pray the words of Psalm 8:1-5:

Chapter 16
Sovereignty of Our Creator

THE TRUTHS WE NEED MOST to reestablish are that of the sovereignty of God and the authority of His Word. We must not waste time denying, puzzling over, or arrogantly trying to disprove who God is or what He has done. The sovereignty of God means "God causes or allows all things to happen that do happen." He is not passively sitting by like a weak, old grandfather with a long, white beard as this world destroys itself. He has been actively involved in His creation from the beginning. He is taking His creation to a destination for a grand purpose. And He had a purpose for creating you and me.

Thornton Wilder framed the question in his novel *The Bridge of San Luis Rey*. Hundreds of people had crossed the rope bridge every day for a century before it collapsed, causing the death of five travelers on July 20, 1714. It had been called "the finest bridge in all Peru."

"Why did this happen to those five?" Wilder has one of his characters ask: "If there were any plan in the universe at all, if there were any pattern in a human life, surely it could be discovered latent in those lives so mysteriously cut off." The author continued, "Either we live by accident and die by accident, or we live by plan and die by plan."

Nothing happens by chance. Ephesians 1:11 says that *God works out everything according to the purpose of His will.* An all-wise, all-powerful God does not need millions of years of chance, mistakes, death, and mutations to create His creation, as theistic evolutionists teach. As stated previously, belief in theistic evolution and the Bible are incompatible. Nor does He allow chance to rule in the life of a believer in Jesus Christ!

Belief in random chance is at the core of the hoax of evolution. But Dr. James Coppedge, an expert in statistical probability, has calculated that the chance of forming a single protein molecule from random processes (even in hundreds of millions of years) is 1 in 10^{161} (10 followed by 161 zeros!). Chance in this sense means "that which happens without a cause." It implies lack of design and of a designer. In his book *Not a Chance: The Myth of Chance in Modern Science and Cosmology,* R. C. Sproul says, "If chance exists in any size, shape, or form, God cannot exist. The two are mutually exclusive. If chance existed, it would destroy God's sovereignty. If God is not sovereign, He is not God. If He is not God, He simply is not. If chance is, God is not. If God is, chance is not."[1]

Proverbs 16:33 says, "The lot is cast into the lap, but its every decision is from the Lord." Maybe we should use this method to settle more disputes (Proverbs 18:18)!

Faith in a sovereign God means we believe He either causes or He allows all things to happen that do happen. Some things that happen are good, some are bad. Some things that *could* happen but do not happen are good, some are bad. He causes some things, He allows some things, and He *prevents* some things (good and bad in themselves) from occurring. He does all this for a good *purpose* in the lives of His children!

RESCUE AND RECOVERY

THINKING IT THROUGH
   Meditate upon the sovereignty of God and belief in chance.
   What do you think of the idea of "luck"? Do you credit
"luck" or God for good things that happen to you?

LISTENING TO GOD
   Ephesians 1:11

   Romans 8:28

   Proverbs 18:18

How does God's viewpoint change your thoughts and actions?

DIGGING OUT
Write out and pray the words of Psalm 86:7-8:

Chapter 17
Hope for Survival

SURVIVING AN AVALANCHE depends upon keeping one's head, for there are only seconds to react. A person cannot outrun an avalanche, nor should he climb into a cave or under a rock ledge. He must swim to the side, shout out for help to inform others of his position, and then close his mouth to keep from being choked by melted snow. He must not try to dig out from underneath the snow unless light is visible, for he will waste precious energy in the dark, cold depths.

National Hope

Is there any hope for America's survival as a nation? Our only national hope is in repentance, rediscovery of our roots and returning to the Biblical standard that made us great as a nation. Alexis de Tocqueville was a French political writer and statesman who toured America in search of the reason for her great success as a nation. In 1835, he wrote a book called *Democracy in America*. Failing to find significant reason for America's prosperity anywhere else, he visited churches across the land. de Tocqueville concluded, "Not until I went into the churches of America and heard her pulpits flame with righteousness did I understand the secret of her genius and power. America is great because America is good, and if America ever ceases to be good, America will cease to be great."[1]

America is already under God's judgment and many do not even realize it! We may have only a short time left to repent and turn to God. But, there is also hope in history. God will relent and hold back the disaster He plans to send upon a nation if that nation repents of its evil (Jeremiah 18:7-10). The Gentile city of

Ninevah repented under Jonah's preaching and so was spared in that generation. God would have spared the entire city of Sodom for the sake of only ten righteous people — but they were not to be found (Genesis 19:32). When righteous King Josiah repented of his nation's sins and led great reforms throughout the land, God postponed judgment until Josiah was dead (II Kings 22:8-20). Judgment still came, for God cannot be mocked. But judgment was *delayed* because of *repentance*. Just after the American Revolution, our nation was in moral and spiritual decline, under an avalanche of sin. Desperate prayer from alarmed Christians led to the Second Great Awakening and great social reform! We like to sing "God Bless America." We need to pray, "God, forgive America" and "God, save America," as we forsake the sins that have caused His judgment to fall upon us. National leaders must lead us to humble ourselves, to seek God's face, to trust the Lord Jesus Christ as Savior, and to turn from pornography, murder of the unborn, pride, greed, and other sins so God's further judgment is delayed.

Personal Hope

Is there any individual hope for men, women, boys, and girls who live in America? So many have no purpose beyond self-gratification, which leaves people so empty. This purposelessness can be fatal.

A chaplain named Gerecke dealt with Nazis in Nuremberg Prison who had killed millions of Jews during World War II. One Nazi chief who refused to accept Christ was Herman Goring. Chaplain Gerecke wrote, "that evening, around 8:30, I had a long session with Goring during which he made sport of the story of creation, ridiculed divine inspiration of the Scriptures, and made outright denial of certain Christian fundamentals." Less than two hours later, he commited suicide! Rejection of the God of creation and of His Word always leaves people without purpose and meaning. If we believe humans are evolving blobs of protoplasm derived from animals and on our way to another stage, we obviously do not believe we are made in God's image. No wonder so many lack purpose.

Those who gain fame and/or wealth in this world without knowing the *purpose* for which God created them stand in grave danger. Examples include Ernest Hemingway, one of history's most famous authors, who was an atheist and died by suicide. Beautiful movie star Marilyn Monroe was idolized by a generation, but she lacked purpose, took drugs, and evidently also died by suicide. Wealthy Howard Hughes, one of the richest men who ever lived, became a hermit and died as a miserable recluse. Money, beauty, and fame can never compensate for lack of God-given purpose in life.

God speaks authoritatively in His Word, which is forever settled in heaven (Psalm 119:89). He plans for this world to be under the personal ruling of Jesus Christ (Ephesians 1:10). Every knee will one day bow to Him, including those in heaven, on earth, and under the earth (Philippians 2:10-11). His eternal purpose was to make known His manifold wisdom (Ephesians 3:10-11). It may not seem so now, but history is "His story" and it moves toward the glory of Jesus Christ (Romans 11:33-36). God's purpose has never changed (Hebrews 6:17), and there are a number of dynamic American churches who still believe and preach God's Word. These groups are thriving in spirit and growing in numbers!

Have you discovered your purpose for living? You will find real, lasting purpose only in a relationship with your Creator. God made us to live with Him forever (II Corinthians 5:5). You were made for His glory (Ephesians 1:12). You were made for the purpose of glorifying God and enjoying Him forever. To "glorify" means "to cause Him to look good in the eyes of others." Our goal in life must be "to please Him" (II Corinthians 5:9). We who believe God are predestined to be adopted as His sons through Jesus Christ (Ephesians 1:5). He will finish what He began in our lives (Philippians 1:6). He causes us both to will and to act according to His good purpose (Philippians 2:13). When we please Him, we will pray continually and stand boldly for righteousness.

The goal of the Apostle Paul was to know Christ and to win heavenly rewards (Philippians 2:7-14). Our goal should be the same. Eternal life is a *gift,* given to us for simply believing God. But *rewards* are given for faithful service to Jesus Christ *after* He has saved us!

Our time is running out. We are far from God and His truth. We can never return to Him by rationalism, which is as old as Plato and ran out of gas a long time ago. God has been seeking our attention for a long time, but maybe He put an exclamation point behind His warning on September 11, 2001.

God's sign warns "Avalanche Ahead" for America and for all who reject Christ. That is because we have swallowed Satan's lies. Our culture says the warning "does not apply to us." Our culture says the warning "discriminates against me and my lifestyle." Our culture says the sign is "outdated" and in the "minority" today, so we do not have to obey it. Almighty God says the opposite.

This American generation may not survive the avalanche of sin and judgment of God. But repentant Americans, like anyone else on earth, can be saved one person at a time!

Will you continue to believe the increasingly Godless culture and remain lost and purposeless?

Or, will you believe God, trusting Jesus Christ to save you and to give you eternal purpose?

RESCUE AND RECOVERY

THINKING IT THROUGH

For what purpose did God create us? What is your purpose in life? Does your purpose match God's purpose for your life?

What are the prospects for America if we repent of our sins?

What do you think will happen if America refuses to repent? What are your prospects for eternity if you refuse to repent of your sin and turn to Christ?

LISTENING TO GOD

Micah 6:8

II Chronicles 7:14

Philippians 2:10-11

How does God's viewpoint change your thoughts and actions?

DIGGING OUT

Write out and pray the words of Psalm 85:4-7:

Selected References

Chapter 2

  1 Hardin, Garrett, *Nature and Man's Fate* (Reinhart and Company, 1959).

  2 Walter, Jeremy, *In Six Days* (Green Forest, Arkansas: Master Books, 2000).

Chapter 3

  1 Hanegraaff, Hank, *The Face* (Nashville: Word Publishing, 1998)

  2 Monod, Jacques, "The Secret of Life," interview with Laurie John, Australian Broadcasting Company, June 10, 1976. As quoted in Hanegraaff, *The Face*. pp. 102-103.

  3 Huxley, Sir Julian, Associated Press dispatch, Address at Darwin Centennial Convocation, Chicago University, November 29, 1959. See Sol Tax, ed., *Issues in Evolution* (Chicago: University of Chicago Press, 1960) p. 252. As quoted in Hank Hanegraaff, *The Face* (Nashville: Word Publishing, 1998) p. 70.

  4 Federer, William, *America's God and Country,* (Coppell, Texas: Fame Publishing, 1994).

Chapter 4

  1 Patterson, Dr. Colin, As quoted by Hanegraaff in *Evolution: Fact, Theory, or FARCE?* (Rancho Santa Margarita, California: Christian Research Institute, 1999).

Chapter 5

  1 LaHaye, Tim and Jenkins, Jerry, *Are We Living in the End Times?* (Wheaton, Illinois: Tyndale House, 1999).

  2 Lamont, Ann, *21 Great Scientists Who Believed the Bible* (Queensland, Australia: Creation Science Foundation, 1995)

  3 Morris, Henry, *Men of Science, Men of God* (Green Forest, Arkansas: Master Books).

  4. Hanegraaff, p. 11.

Chapter 6

  1 Keith, Sir Arthur, *Evolution and Ethics* (New York: Putman, 1947) p. 230.

Chapter 7

  1 Darwin, Charles, *The Descent of Man in Relation to Sex* (New York: D. Appleton and Co., 1896) p. 564. As quoted in Scott Klusendorf, *Pro-Life 101* (Signal Hill, California: Stand to Reason Press, 2002) p. 33.

  2 Cited in Stephen Jay Gould, The Mismeasure of Man (New York: Norton, 1981) pp. 104-105. As quoted in Scott Klusendorf, *Pro-Life 101* (Signal Hill, California: Stand to Reason Press, 2002) pp. 33-34).

  3 Witham, Larry, "Darwinisn may explain Clinton's trysts", *(Washington Times,* August 24, 1998) Section A, p A8.

Chapter 9

1 Howe, J., *The Changing Political Thought of John Adams*, as cited by Gary DeMar in *You've Heard It Said.* (Brentwood, Tennessee: Wolgemuth and Hyatt, 1991) p. 95.

2 Harris, Eric, As cited by Frank Peretti in *Wounded Spirit* (Nashville: Word Publishing, 2000).

Chapter 16

1 Sproul, R. C. *Not a Chance: The Myth of Chance in Modern Science and Cosmology.* (Grand Rapids, Michigan: Baker Books, 1994) p. 9.

Chapter 17

1 deTocqueville, Alexis, *Democracy in America* (1835).

Appendices

I. The Problem and The Solution

II. God's Great Rescue

III. Spiritual Temperature Test

Appendix I
The Problem and the Solution

The Problem:

"EVOLUTION" (MOLECULES-TO-MAN) — along with its millions of years — actually equates to this: "man's opinions determine truth" (i.e., these ideas do not in any way originate from the Bible).

If man believes he can determine his origins without revelation from God, then ultimately he can justify anything he can get away with in society.

Abortion, pornography, homosexual behavior, etc., aren't caused by "evolution" or belief in millions of years. But the more someone accepts ideas such as millions of years (with death/bloodshed *before* sin) that undermine the Bible's history, the more they can justify in their own mind that they can do whatever they want.

The castle structure of man deciding truth is built on the philosophical foundation of evolution/millions of years — man not answerable to a higher authority.

Christianity is built on the foundation that the Bible's history is true. The Creation/Fall/Flood accounts of Genesis 1-11 are foundational to the rest of the Bible — to every doctrine — and to Christian morality.

Humanists know that to destroy Christianity, it's best not to aim directly at its structure (e.g., the doctrine of the resurrection) but, instead, to attack its foundation. Their efforts through the education system, media, etc., have convinced vast numbers (sadly, including most church leaders) that the Genesis account is not "real" history. Thus, we see the collapse of Christian morality — the increasing abortion, pornography, lawlessness, marriage breakdown, etc.

The Church desperately tries to deal with these issues, but they are just the *symptoms* of the real problem, which is the loss of the real foundation for the Christian structure — and its replacement in society by a man-centered foundation.

The Solution:

THE CHURCH NEEDS TO UNDERSTAND, and fight, the battle at this foundational level. It needs to restore the foundation of the authority of God's Word beginning with Genesis. The church must answer the skeptical questions of the age that attack the Bible's history, and show that this history (which encompasses all of reality — death, disease, dinosaurs, geology, biology, etc.) *can* be trusted and is confirmed by real science.

As the true foundation is restored and the wrong foundation eroded away, the correct structure (the Christian worldview) can be built, and the wrong structure, which exalts itself against the knowledge of God, can be torn down (II Corinthians 10:5).

Ken Ham, President
Answers in Genesis

Appendix II
God's Great Rescue

PERHAPS YOU HAVE READ this book, but never personally trusted the Savior with your earthly life and your eternal destiny. The following explains how God has provided
for your eternal rescue through Jesus Christ:

ILLUSTRATION #1
GOD CREATED YOU, KNOWS YOU INTI-
MATELY, AND LOVES YOU.

A. GOD CREATED YOU.

*So God created man in His own im-
age, in the image of God He created
him; male and female He created them.*
Genesis 1:27

*For You created my inmost being,
You knit me together in my mother's
womb.*
Psalm 139:13

B. GOD KNOWS YOU INTIMATELY.
*You know when I sit and when I rise;
You perceive my thoughts from afar.
You discern my going out and my lying down;
You are familiar with all my ways.
Before a word is on my tongue
You know it completely, O Lord.*
Psalm 139:2-4

C. GOD LOVES YOU.
*For God so loved the world that He
gave His one and only Son, that
whoever believes in Him shall not
perish but have eternal life.*
John 3:16

ILLUSTRATION #2

We are covered up in an avalanche of sin. All of us are sinners and separated from God. He is perfect, pure, and good; we are not. All our good works, philosophy, and religion cannot reach God. Because by nature we disobey Him and resist Him, He cannot have fellowship with us without denying His goodness and holiness. Instead, He must judge us.

A. You Are a Sinner.

For all have sinned and fall short of the glory of God. . . .

Romans 3:23

B. Sin Separates You from a Holy God.

For your iniquities have separated you from your God; your sins have hidden His face from you . . .

Isaiah 59:2

C. Eternal Punishment Is the Penalty for Sin.

For the wages of sin is death. . . .

Romans 6:23

If anyone's name was not found written in the book of life, he was thrown into the lake of fire.

Revelation 20:15

ILLUSTRATION #3

God sent His only Son, Jesus Christ, to rescue you from sin and death by taking your punishment on the cross! Only He can give you new life and peace with God.

A. GOD SENT HIS SON.

But God demonstrates His own love for us in this: while we were still sinners, Christ died for us.
Romans 5:8

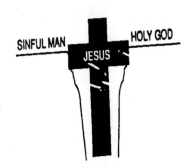

B. CHRIST DIED IN OUR PLACE.

For Christ died for sin once for all, the righteous for the unrighteous, to bring you to God.
I Peter 3:18

C. HE IS THE ONLY WAY TO GOD.

Jesus answered, "I am the Way and the Truth and the Life. No one comes to the Father except through Me."
John 14:6

119

ILLUSTRATION #4

You *must trust* in the sacrifice of Christ as payment in full for your sin and *personally accept* God's graceful forgiveness.

A. YOU MUST TRUST CHRIST.

Believe in the Lord Jesus, and you will be saved. . . .

Acts 16:31

Yet to all who received Him, to those who believed in His name, He gave the right to become children of God. . . .

John 1:12

B. HIS DEATH IS PAYMENT IN FULL FOR ALL YOUR SIN.

. . . justified freely by His grace through the redemption that came by Christ Jesus.

Romans 3:24

Therefore, there is now no condemnation for those who are in Christ Jesus. . . .

Romans 8:1

C. SALVATION IS BY GRACE AND NOT BY WORKS.

However, to the man who does not work but trusts God who justifies the wicked, his faith is credited as righteousness.

Romans 4:5

For it is by grace you have been saved, through faith — and this not from yourselves, it is the gift of God — not by works, so that no one can boast.

Ephesians 2:8-9

Why not receive Jesus Christ as your Savior and Lord right now? Simply say: "Yes, Lord," to His offer to forgive you for your sins and to change you.

_____

(signed)

_____

(date)

Tell someone of your decision and keep studying God's Word. These things greatly strengthen you (Romans 10:9-10). You may write *Winning Run Foundation* for further encouragement. We would be thrilled to hear of your commitment! Welcome to eternal life!

WINNING RUN FOUNDATION
One University Avenue
Bourbonnais, IL 60914

Appendix III
Spiritual Temperature Test

PART I: KNOWLEDGE

1. How do you know there is a God?

2. What do we know about the nature of God?

3. What is the nature of mankind? How do you know?

4. According to Romans 10:9-10, how do people gain a right relationship to God?

5. Define "truth" using John 14:6 and John 17:17.

6. What are the two major worldviews concerning the source of truth? (See 1 John 4:1-6)

7. Upon what is the scientific method based?

8. Who was the only One present when human history began? (See John 1:1-5)

9. Should one's belief in how humanity began be based upon faith or upon observation? (Hebrews 11:3)

10. How do you know Scripture is reliable?

11.What are three steps in the inductive study of Scripture?

    a.

    b.

    c.

12. What is a stronghold?

13. What does one's view of origins have to do with his
or her behavior?

14. State three reasons why some people continue to
believe we evolved from "molecules to man" over millions
of years.

    a.

    b.

    c.

15. Why is belief in theistic evolution a threat to one's
spiritual health?

16. When did death originate? (Romans 5)

17. When did God separate people into nations? How
did He do it? Why did He do it?

18. What is the difference between religion and a relationship with God?

19. Define the "sovereignty of God."

20. Why are those who refuse to believe God not able to comprehend truth? (Romans 1:18, 28)

BONUS QUESTION
For what purpose were we created? (Ephesians 1:12)

PART II: APPLICATION

1. Which phrase best describes your personal, daily plan for communication with God?
    a. A minimum of 10 minutes of uninterrupted prayer and Bible study early every morning.
    b. A brief verse and sentence prayer whenever convenient.
    c. No plan for daily communication with God.

2. If your answer above is "c," what is the major reason you have no daily communication with God?
    a. I am too busy to talk to and listen to God.
    b. I do not think communicating with God is important.
    c. I do not believe God talks to people today.

3. What is your plan for communicating to others that they can go to heaven by trusting in the Lord Jesus Christ?
    a. I often share my experience with Christ and explain God's plan using an outline similar to "God's Great Rescue" in Appendix II.
    b. I live a good life and hope others will ask me about Jesus.
    c. I never communicate anything to anybody about God's plan to save all who repent of sin.

4. If your answer above is "b," how many people have asked you to tell them about Jesus and God's plan of salvation?
    a. So many I have lost count.
    b. One person several years ago.
    c. No one has ever asked me about Jesus and Heaven.

5. If your answer above is "c," why do you not take the initiative?

    a. I do not know how to explain salvation and refuse to learn.

    b. I hope someone else will tell them before it is too late.

    c. I just do not want to tell anyone about Jesus.

6. Which statement best describes your attitude toward life?

    a. I totally yield my will to God's will and daily submit to His control.

    b. I want God to take me to heaven when I die, but I insist upon controlling my own life while on earth.

    c. Sometimes I submit to God's will and some times I demand my own way.

7. If your answer is "b" or "c" above, read Romans 6 and 7 and write a short response. If your answer is "a," read Romans 8 and outline the benefits.

8. How do you give and receive encouragement to joyfully continue your walk with Jesus Christ?

    a. I regularly attend a church where God's Word is believed and taught and there is joy in worship.

    b. I occasionally find encouragement from somone.

    c. I refuse to attend church because I need no encouragement.

9. If your answer above is "c," how are you doing?
   a. I always live joyfully above all circumstances.
   b. I am sometimes discouraged and inconsistent in my Christian life.
   c. I am often discouraged and need to find a joyful assembly of Jesus' followers.

10. Write a short paragraph describing your plan to apply what you have learned in this book.

RESOURCES

A WISE MAN once said that the most backward child who possesses and believes God's Word knows more truth than the educated intellectual who disbelieves the Word of God.

Hundreds of qualified scientists believe in the historical accuracy and authority of God's Word from the very first verse. These scientific creationists not only believe God's Word, but also that the evidence of true science confirms its validity and disproves the evolutionary hypotheses. Though ridiculed by those scientists who reject God and His Word, their arguments are compelling.

There are at least seventy-five creationist organizations in America and thirty overseas which promote Biblical creationism.

Listed below are three organizations which provide many videos, books, and magazines written by creation scientists:

1. **ANSWERS IN GENESIS**
   P. O. Box 6330
   Florence, KY 41022

   www.answersingenesis.org

2. **INSTITUTE FOR CREATION RESEARCH**
   P. O. Box 2667
   El Cajon, CA 92021

   1-800-628-7640

3. **VISION FORUM MINISTRIES**
   4719 Blanco Road
   San Antonio, TX 78212

   www.visionforum.org